Introducing Ralph K. Manley

Anyone who has met Ralph K. Manley recognizes him as that inspiring, enthusiastic, positive man who is always "raring to go." However, many may wonder, "Is this the real Ralph K.?"

I have had the privilege of working with Mr. Manley since I invited him to teach real estate courses at Southwest Missouri State University (now Missouri State University) thirty-five years ago. He was delighted not only to teach the students but also to inspire them to strive for their potential. At the same time, he enthusiastically worked together with his colleagues and me in the best interest of the department and the university.

Between 1978 and 1992, Ralph and I took eight groups of students to New York as part of the New York Corporate/Financial Study. Each time, for eight days, he and I and a student or faculty member shared a suite in Manhattan's Salisbury Hotel. Consequently, we were together for two-hundred hours, operating under a demanding and strenuous schedule. Ralph K. never deviated from being that inspiring, enthusiastic, positive man—always "raring to go"!

Vencil J. Bixler
Former Chair of Business Department
(Southwest) Missouri State University

We grew up in a home where "All days are good, some are just better than others" was our motto. We were not allowed to have a bad day, because no matter how bad we felt our day was, we were reminded that there were many, many people having a much worse day. If we were dreading a test, and lamenting the day, Dad would always say, "No, no, all days are good, some are just better than others."

This was not just a phrase to him; it was a lifestyle. Despite being reared in a broken home, separated from his twin brother while he went to live and work on his grandparents' farm, then going into WWII as a paratrooper, he still believed that God had given him so many gifts. He believed a positive attitude (along with a lot of hard work) was the key to obtaining everything anyone could want out of life.

In his eighties, you might think we would try to dissuade him from traveling the world, jumping out of airplanes, and steering clear of high ladders putting up his Christmas lights. But, just as we can't easily stop a freight train, we do not stand in the way of Dad. He is still a very driven man who believes in God and hard work and-more than anything-having a positive attitude.

As I have gotten older, I have heard myself say to my children, "All days are good, some are just better than others!" I know that, as much as it used to irritate me as a child, the attitude has stuck with me and, God willing, will pass on to future generations.

What better legacy to pass to your grandchildren than the knowledge that life is good!

Jennifer Manley Davis

Many years ago I met Ralph Manley while he was teaching in the Continuing Education Department at Drury University. Because I was completely charmed by his exciting personality, I decided I wanted to know more about him. I found out that he was a Builder and Developer of beautiful apartments and other structures. I also learned that he served our nation in WWII and had been serving our city of Springfield ever since.

In all these years since, I have become very close to this important man. I have followed his outstanding career, have had the opportunity to serve with him on various Boards of Directors, and am always amazed by his energy and his compassion. He is, and has been, a shining light in our city for a lifetime.

James R. (Jim) Craig
Past President, Board of Governors,
(Southwest) Missouri State University

In our lives we interact with others, both on a personal and professional basis, who will have an impact on us in many different ways. Those who set a good example with their selflessness, integrity and morals cause us to try to emulate them. Those who demonstrate fortitude and are sincerely spiritual will also make us want to try and mirror their same fine examples. Ralph K. Manley has always demonstrated all of these fine qualities.

I first met him twenty-nine years ago when he was a professor of finance at MSU (formerly SMSU). I knew then that I wanted to be in banking and help others, as he did in so many different ways.

As a veteran who understands, Ralph teaches everyone to appreciate and respect those who have fought for our freedom and liberty. As a self-made, very successful entrepreneur, he has worked hard and smart to accomplish what he has achieved, always setting his goals a little bit higher. As a city leader, he wants us to appreciate our community and he shows by example how to make it a better place to live and grow. As a great man, he makes us want to strive to be better people.

Mr. Manley has played a large part in my professional and personal development because I've tried to be a little more like him.

> David M. Thater,
> Senior Vice President
> Citizens National Bank of Springfield

THE SKY IS THE LIMIT

The Autobiography of Ralph K. Manley

By Ralph K. Manley

As told to and
written by
Susie Knust

Birch Creek Publishing
Marshfield, Missouri
2006

The Sky is the Limit
The Autobiography of Ralph K. Manley

By Ralph K. Manley

**As told to and written by
Susie Knust**

Published by:
Birch Creek Publishing
P.O. Box 777
Marshfield, MO 65706-0777
www.birchcreekpublishing.com

Dedication

To my wonderful wife, Jayne, who has been with and supported me through the good times and the bad;

To my children, Janell, Jodell, and Jennifer, who are the light of my life;

To my brother, Roland, whose life and death left an indelible print on my heart;

To my friends, including those in business, church, and education, who have personally inspired me;

Without all of these people, my story would not have been possible.

Dust Jacket Painting:
"101st Airborne: Hour of Liberation"
Larry Selman, artist
lselman@supernet.com

Book layout and design by Steven Ross
sr-graphics@earthlink.net

Printed by Litho Printers, Cassville, Missouri, U.S.A.

Contents

Contents

Introduction

Just because you might be poor today doesn't mean you have to stay poor. Just because you might be injured, physically or emotionally, doesn't mean you can't develop your skills and be very successful, and also be a contributing factor to the happiness and success of many other people.

There is hope for everyone! All you need to have is a dream, be willing to work for it, and develop a good saving ethic. More than ever before, these are essential to greater joy in life. Hard work and not spending all you earn are not to be dreaded; they accomplish your dreams!

This is an age of specialization, and each of us can contribute to a higher standard of living for all of us.

If you read this, about what's happened to a little boy from Springfield, Missouri, who achieved a dream to become a builder, a developer of residential properties, and has enjoyed it, maybe you will understand that you need to do what you enjoy and what comes easiest for you, in order to be a success in life. But do it well and strive to be the best in your field!

Most of all, I hope the story of my life will instill in all who read it: the door to opportunity opens its widest in America, and education is the key.

RKM

Part I

WORLD WAR II

It was shortly after midnight and all hell had broken loose in what looked like the biggest Fourth of July celebration imaginable. There were tracers, and the Germans shot up parachute flares.

My plane took a lot of hits, as did some of the people in the plane. Several had fallen to the floor. Some had gotten sick. The floor was slick with blood and vomit.

We were already hooked up to the static line ready to jump as the bullets were flying.

When it was my turn, I was number three out the door–thankful to escape. Some of the soldiers didn't get out. I watched the plane go on to crash.

For sixty days I fought in Normandy, France. I went on to see action in Operation "Market Garden" in Holland, where the Dutch Resistance made the German defeat much less difficult.

Then I joined the rest of the 101st in the Belgian town of Bastogne. We were surrounded for days, outnumbered by the Germans 20 to 1 before defeating them on the 26th of December 1944.

I earned two Bronze Stars and five Purple Hearts while serving my country for three years during World War Two.

D-Day Jump

I was a paratrooper in the 501st Parachute Infantry Regiment, part of the 101st Airborne Division. Both my twin brother, Roland, and I enlisted in the Army halfway through our senior year at Springfield High School, in 1942. Young people wanted to go in the service because everybody else did. It was a patriotic thing to do. We both wanted to be Airborne, which offered pay three times that of an average private. The Army had a policy against placing twins together. So Roland went into the 82nd Airborne Division and I went into the 101st.

Roland earned his paratrooper wings first and in July 1943 was dispatched to North Africa to prepare for a jump into Sicily. But Roland's plane was one of eighteen shot down in friendly fire over the Mediterranean Sea, mistaken for Germans by our Navy.

The Army offered to send me home because of my brother's death. But, I'd be laughed at–classified a 4-F, unfit for military service. I chose not to come home! I wanted to get revenge on the powers responsible for this war. My first chance came nearly a year later in my first combat action: the D-Day invasion.

I was 20 years old. I waddled onto my C-47 in England on June 5, 1944 and stepped on a scale to record my weight: I weighed 417 pounds with all the equipment. Normally a paratrooper would have 75 to 100 pounds, but they wanted us to take everything we needed to do our job. Being a demolitionist I had—

-50 lbs. of 2.5-lb. explosives in two 25-lb. bags fastened to my legs;
-fuses, primer cord, blasting caps and a detonator for the explosives;
-three 10-lb. antitank mines;
-an 85-lb. flamethrower and gelatinized gasoline;
-a folding-stock carbine weapon and 100 rounds of ammunition;

-six hand grenades, a .45-cal. pistol and 50 rounds of ammunition;

-three knives: one on my left, one in my collar, a smaller one on my ankle;

-a cricket clicker for identification;

-main parachute on my back, reserve parachute on my front;

-three boxes of K-rations;

-rope, shovel, helmet, flashlight, field glasses, canteen of water, halizone pills to purify water, "Mae West" life preserver;

-Musette bag with socks, personal items, three condoms (useful for keeping mud and sand out of rifle barrels);

-French francs printed in America (about $25 worth);

-First-aid packets, including one containing morphine.

It was 12:23 a.m., just after midnight, on June 6, 1944, over Normandy, France, and the anti-aircraft fire was intense. Every fifth bullet was a tracer bullet, trailing a stream of fire behind it, so those shooting could tell where the bullets were going. These tracer bullets were going through the airplane.

With our static lines hooked up to a cable in the plane, we had to stay in sequence: one, two, three, four, five, so on. The fifteen-foot-long static line, a large canvas strap with the hook fastener, was fastened at its other end to the pinnacle, the peak, of the parachute.

We had hooked on the fastener to the cable in the plane and slid it down, one man after another, to the door. The door was open; in fact, it was off, and stored inside the plane.

We got a red light when we were getting near the drop zone, and then once we got to the drop zone, we got the green light. That's when we jumped out.

The C-47 airplane, a twin-engine plane, was noisy, but in addition to the open rear door, there were other planes besides the plane that I was in. All this noise and the anti-aircraft fire made it intensely loud.

Some of the people were hit in the plane, fell to the floor, and could not get out.

Just before I jumped, my plane was hit by German fire and burst into flames.

I was the third man to jump from the burning craft. I found out later: two more jumped behind me but the sixth soldier was shot in the doorway. His cables trapped the rest of the crew, blocked the doorway, and all thirteen remaining died when the plane crashed. I jumped at about 200 feet above ground, my chute opened, then I hit the ground. I watched the rest of my men crash about one-half mile away.

I did not land on our Drop Zone. Most people didn't because some planes diverted their paths to avoid the anti-air-craft fire that was so intense, and some of the pathfinders lit right in the middle of an enemy camp!

Pathfinders were the troops who jumped earlier before our groups so they could direct the planes either by way of radar or green lights or red lights, something to attract to a certain spot on the ground, so we wouldn't miss the Drop Zone. Then once we landed, they were responsible for any different way that was already specified for a particular group to get together, to assemble on, like eagle calls or dog calls.

Because it was a nighttime jump, we couldn't see to guide ourselves. I found out later that some landed on church steeples, trees, barns, houses. Some others were captured the moment they landed on the ground.

Where I hit the ground I was in about a foot of mud and water. My training kicked in: the first objective was to get out of the parachute and abandon it, because it was merely a means of transportation to get there; it had no other value or use for me. The next objective: get oriented as to where I was, by sounds, maybe a railroad or the highway; by sight, maybe a church steeple, so I could go to my military objectives.

The Germans had shot up parachute flares, white parachutes with a fire burning underneath them, which really lit the whole countryside. It enabled them to just scintillate troopers and planes. I saw those and knew that we were in for fighting!

Some of the houses were on fire. When a tracer bullet hit a thatched roof, it set it on fire. That silhouetted things also. Some of the livestock were already killed, because of the shells and bombing from the air force and the navy.

These were little communities that had many little pastures for cattle and livestock. The hedgerows themselves had grown up higher than the fields because for years the fields had been farmed. With the scattered dropping and with the small fields, I couldn't see beyond any one field. I'd have to go to the hedgerow itself and kind of peek over to see or hear anything. Because this was June and the spring growth had come on, some of the hedgerows were so thick that I might be on one side of a hedgerow and some Germans on the other!

In every field there would be a gate to get in, but most of them were zeroed in on by the Germans. Maybe they hadn't been before we got there, but they were now! So I didn't dare go to the open gate to leave that field to go to another.

I was really loaded down with everything I would need. The Musette bag that was normally carried on our back was put on our front, below our reserve parachute when we jumped, because our big chute was on the back. So after I got rid of my parachutes, on the ground, and got out of the harness, then I had to make the adjustment to put the Musette bag with the other personal things on my back.

The Germans had flooded a lot of the areas of the open fields by opening the locks on the canals, trying to keep us from landing there, particularly with gliders. Gliders were to bring in the heavier equipment, as well as jeeps and artillery pieces, besides the glider infantry troops and re-supply. Paratroopers' equipment that we didn't have on us came in by glider.

There were lots of little canals there, branches of canals, and it seemed like one was about five feet wide and about five feet deep. The explosives I was carrying were such that, when I'd run to try to jump over this five-foot-wide canal–I could jump five feet, I could jump ten feet, but jumping five feet over the top of a little canal all loaded down–I'd run one way and the motion of my legs running caused the bags heavy with explosives to swing, and when I stopped running to jump over the canal, the bags were still swinging and I landed right in the middle of the canal!

About five feet deep! And it seemed the sides were nearly straight so I had to go to a place where I could get a hold of a clump of grass or something to try and pull myself out. I ended up soaking wet, obviously, but it didn't really bother the explosives, because we had detonators and fuses. Water didn't hamper me!

I couldn't see what was human, what was our own, what was enemy, what was livestock. It was very difficult to tell! I believe the first sound I heard was livestock; they were running because they were scared, with the troops landing. I could tell, by the silhouettes, a horse from a cow. There was no moon; it was dark except for the tracers and the Germans' parachute flares. My eyes and ears were what kept me alive, and warned me, let me know, of anybody, any motion, whether cow or horse or sheep or enemy or truck or tank. And once a shell would burst, it put out some light and I could see exactly what an object was.

Being a demolitionist, my first military objective was to disrupt communications. Next, we demolitionists were to put anti-tank mines on the roads–they were about ten pounds apiece. We used what we called a daisy chain. We fastened a small wire on a rope, and as something coming down the road got to us, the little wire would pull the rope and the rope would pull the mine across. That way whoever was coming could not see the mine. We'd have a foxhole on either side, with some of the other people manning the foxholes.

Next we were to put explosives on the railroad tracks, because in some cases the Germans would bring out the large artillery pieces mounted on railroad cars and fire, then take them back into tunnels or trees, where we couldn't see them. We were to blow the railroad tracks, if we had to.

After that we were to go after the pillboxes. Some of the pillboxes were dome-shaped, and bombs and shells from the Air Force or Navy might just bounce off of them or merely take nicks out of them. But, if we went around to the front of those, then we could shoot the flamethrower inside the opening where the gun barrel came out and that would kill everybody inside. If it didn't burn them alive, it would burn all the oxygen and they would suffocate.

Another of our D-Day assignments was to put explosives on the bridges, so that if the Germans came with their armor or troops or reinforcements, we could blow the bridges to keep them from coming down.

We did blow up bridges, but we put explosives on a number that we did not blow up. It was only when we were threatened.

Because the Germans had flooded the flat areas to discourage or hamper the gliders or anybody coming in, we wanted the higher ground, which would be the roads. So we wanted to get to the roads. Across a field of mud was no place for a tank or truck to go, and it wasn't really desirable for troops to go.

Also, in some of the open fields there were what we called Rommel's Asparagus, trees they had cut, six to eight inches in diameter and eight to ten feet tall, and planted in the ground like posts. They had strung wire from one to the other, top to top, so that if gliders or planes tried to land there, in these flooded fields, they would crash. Rommel's Asparagus would wreck them. That's what they were for.

Rommel, of course, was the notorious German tank commander for that area. But he had gone to Berlin for his wife's birthday and was not there on D-Day.

D-Day did catch the Germans by surprise, there's no question about it. They knew we were coming but they didn't know when or where, so they were all up and down the coast. Still, we were not sure just how many men and how much material the Germans had there.

The fact that we missed our Drop Zones and were scattered worked to our advantage inasmuch as the Germans thought there were a million of us! We were everywhere but not in large groups. And not intentionally!

Marshaling for D-Day: Two Days Before

To get us ready for D-Day, they took us to a marshaling area at an airport in England–near Exeter, at Greenham Common Airdrome–where the airplanes were located, our C-47 planes out of which we were to jump.

It was almost like a penitentiary in that it had wiring around it. Nobody could get in and nobody could get out except those who were already there. They did not want the enemy to get any news or any idea that the invasion was about to start.

I'm told that in a penitentiary, if a person is to be put to death, he is given a last meal of whatever he'd like. Well, they did that to us there: they gave us a roast chicken, believe it or not, and ice cream and milk. We had not had that for the whole time we'd been in England; it was a fabulous feast.

Some of the fellow soldiers got nervous. Some were eager, much like a horse at the starting gate: we're ready to go, so open the gate and let's get with it! Others were solemn or were offering prayer. Some were sleeping. Some were just joyous and laughing.

Part of what had us in a great mood was that General Eisenhower, who later became President, came and spoke to us. And for a young boy twenty years of age, from this little town of Springfield, Missouri, being greeted by and shaking hands with General Eisenhower–what a situation that was. He wished us good luck and asked where we were from–our hometowns–that type of thing.

We were supposed to go on the 5th of June, but the water in the English Channel was so rough that all those troops that were going by ships would get too seasick. So they postponed the invasion for one day, until the morning of the 6th of June, to give the waters a chance to calm, which they did, some. Prime Minister Churchill, of England, came and spoke to us then, and what a thrill it was to see somebody else of such magnitude.

Because of the combined impact of the Churchill visit and the Eisenhower visit, we young people were now so psyched up we thought, "Well, somebody may get hurt but it isn't going to be me; I can do it; we can handle this!"

We loaded the planes from this marshaling area on the night of the June 5th, between nine and ten o'clock.

General Eisenhower was not sure we were going to be able to stay there, in France, because he actually wrote two speeches: one was his announcing that the Normandy Invasion was on, and the other was his taking the blame for the failure it created. Of course, that second speech never occurred, thank goodness.

We didn't know any of this at the time; some of those facts didn't come out until much later, years later.

Early Encounters and Assembling

I was totally alone when I first landed. With the cattle running around, I couldn't tell if it was also some of my buddies. If I heard a noise and pressed my cricket, it didn't tell me if the noise was a cow, the enemy, a sheep. So I got ready to shoot! And if there was another cricket sound, I couldn't tell from where the sound was coming.

Because D-Day was a nighttime jump, we needed something like the cricket. Though they added to the confusion and didn't really work, they were probably as good as anything we could have used. I stayed under cover until daylight because I couldn't see. And I used the challenge words we'd been given, lightning and thunder.

If I challenged someone I'd whisper "lightning," and if he'd respond "thunder," then I'd know he was an American. But he was not necessarily one from my company or even one from my regiment; we were scattered all over because the planes had veered to avoid anti-aircraft fire.

We were everywhere, which confused the Germans, yes, but we were in very small groups and we were not well organized.

At daylight, I found somebody from my group and we were able to see others who were killed or injured or ready to go but just looking for more of their company. So it probably took a couple of days for many of us to get to our company, as we had planned at the marshaling area.

Everyone on my plane was a demolitionist, and that was a mistake. Because most of the other demolitionists on my plane didn't survive the D-Day jump, we couldn't assemble as a group. It just didn't happen like training! We had to do the job with someone else.

But we learned from our mistakes. After Normandy, they divided us up and put some demolition people in each company. The army learned.

The first person I saw get killed was a Master Sergeant from

Regimental Headquarters. He was next to a rock wall and a shell had hit the rock wall, an artillery shell, and killed him instantly. So I learned right away: don't get on the "coming" side of a brick wall. And not under a tree. And not out in the open.

We didn't dig a foxhole immediately because we didn't know where to dig!

We captured a large group of German paratroopers who had come to try to overtake us, but were actually training right then and walked into us by accident. They waved a flag and put down their weapons. As we took them prisoner and corralled them and were marching down the road–there were probably a hundred captured German paratroopers–the Germans from a long distance off, not knowing it was mainly their troops, started shelling us with their 88 artillery pieces.

Here came the shells! We could hear them!

There were just three of us marching them down the road to an old barn and corral, and we had to go for the ditches on each side of the road. I might be lying on top of a German or one might be lying on top of me, or end to end! Just a low recession in the ground was enough to protect us from the shrapnel.

Before it was over, we arrived with just half of the prisoners because the rest of them were killed or wounded and couldn't march.

It was not our job, really, to guard prisoners; it was our job to keep the Germans from coming down. So until we could get our troops who were coming ashore to guard them and handle the prisoners, we kept them only a short time until they did get ashore and we met them.

That was my first injury but it was just shrapnel in my leg, not enough to disable me. None of my injuries were; I was wounded six times. Most of them were the legs and arms, all shrapnel. Never a bullet, thank goodness.

I could kind of protect myself from bullets by moving fast all the time, being hard to hit, but shrapnel goes anyplace.

When the shell explodes, it breaks into thousands of pieces of metal, all kinds of sharp pieces, and it's hot. When it hits, it kind of sears the wound so there's not really a lot of bad bleeding. I just picked out the metal, because it burns, and put some sulfa powder on the wound, bandaged it, and went on.

Part of the time I got all the metal out. I still have some but it's deeper, and that's one of the things that always trips the security alarm at the airports. And there couldn't be a more patriotic person go through that thing!

We were a very versatile type of troop. When we were dropped behind enemy lines, we had to improvise, because we had no vehicles; we had no means of transportation. Our parachute was our means to get there but once we were on the ground, that was abandoned and we had to seek other things. We had to be very careful.

I found out that I landed somewhere between Carentan and St. Come-Du-Mont on that D-Day jump.

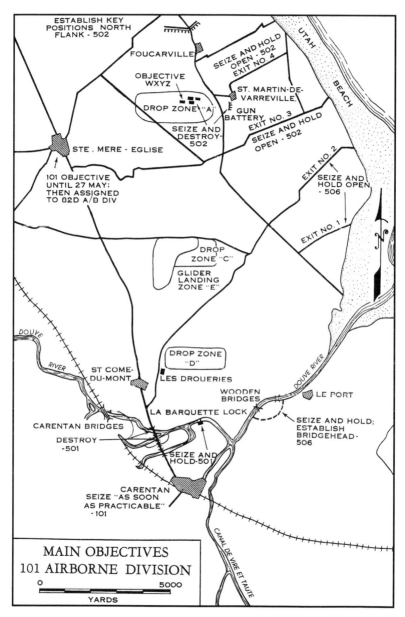

ESTABLISH KEY
POSITIONS NORTH
FLANK - 502

FOUCARVILLE

SEIZE AND HOLD
OPEN - 502
EXIT NO. 4

UTAH BEACH

OBJECTIVE
WXYZ

DROP ZONE "A"

ST. MARTIN-DE-
VARREVILLE.
GUN
BATTERY
EXIT NO. 3

SEIZE AND HOLD
OPEN - 502

SEIZE AND
DESTROY-
502

STE . MERE - EGLISE

101 OBJECTIVE
UNTIL 27 MAY:
THEN ASSIGNED
TO 82D A/B DIV

EXIT NO. 2

SEIZE AND
HOLD OPEN
- 506

EXIT NO. 1

DROP
ZONE "C"

GLIDER
LANDING
ZONE "E"

DOUVE

RIVER

ST COME-
DU-MONT

DROP ZONE
"D"

LES DROUERIES

DOUVE RIVER

WOODEN
BRIDGES

LE PORT

LA BARQUETTE LOCK

SEIZE AND HOLD:
ESTABLISH
BRIDGEHEAD-
506

CARENTAN BRIDGES

DESTROY
-501

SEIZE AND
HOLD-501

CARENTAN
SEIZE "AS SOON
AS PRACTICABLE"
- 101

CANAL DE VIRE ET TAUTE

MAIN OBJECTIVES
101 AIRBORNE DIVISION

0   5000

YARDS

"I found out I landed somewhere between Carentan and
St. Come-Du-Mont on that D-Day jump."

"Our parachute was our means to get there.
Here's a front and back view of a fully equipped paratrooper."

Part of our equipment was invasion money so we could pay people to help or to inform us. And they would certainly be receptive to that.

The French Underground was quite a pipeline between the Americans in England and the French people. They had regular communication to share who, what, where, supplying important information. We had lost quite a number of airplanes, shot down by the Germans. Many times the pilot and crew were able to parachute out and would be hidden and protected by the French, if at all possible, including hiding their parachutes. Then during the nighttime hours the French would get our people to a place where they could get back to England in some way or another. If not, they would have been taken prisoners, of course.

It seemed the French had known something was going to come. Many of the influential French people had been moved out or had moved on their own because they weren't sympathetic with the German cause. So we didn't normally have very many friendly French people in the Normandy area and as we would progress along, some of our troops were killed in house-to-house fighting.

Death and Destruction

What a useless thing it was, to be able to tear down, destroy, and then move forward. Or, from all the automatic weapons, to have the tracer bullets with the fire streaming behind them, setting on fire a thatched roof, or curtains or bedding inside a home. We hated to see all that!

Elmer Neumann was the first one of our group killed on D-Day. He was much like me, a young boy just out of high school, didn't smoke, didn't drink, didn't gamble, but he did enjoy life. He was a happy person! We shared many experiences, especially while in training.

A machine gun opened up on us as we were going across an open space, and here was a large shell hole. I dove for the shell hole, as I'd dive into a swimming pool, and Neumann jumped into the shell hole, standing up and jumping into it, and he was hit as square between the eyes as could be, with one of the shells from the machine gun. And of course he immediately died. So that was the first one of my buddies that was killed.

Why did one dive in the hole and one jump in the hole? It's just whatever we thought at the time. Certainly we had been trained that the lower we were to the ground, the better chance we had of avoiding bullets, or shrapnel for that matter. If we'd get in a hole, the bullets would go over the top of us. In this case, he jumped and was upright and I dove which was almost level with the ground, into this shell hole, and that was the difference between living and not living.

Another close buddy who was killed early on was a fellow named Lorrance, from Lebanon, Missouri. As we were going across an open field, here was a barbed wire fence, and guns opened up on us, so again I dove to go underneath the wire and he straddled the wire to get across, and he took a number of bullets; it was instant death for him, because he was exposed standing up, straddling this barbed wire to get across it. Once again, that just made the difference between living and dying.

A buddy named Porter was hit by shrapnel, all in the stomach, cutting his stomach open, and there were his intestines coming out. What a horrible sight! And he said, "Manley, can you help me? Can you help me?" Immediately, I took the morphine supplied in my first aid kit. That was the first thing we always did, unless we could find a medic, and we couldn't find a medic there, so we gave him a shot of morphine and put the intestines back in, and said, "You're covered! We're going to get you through this!" and so on, but of course we didn't; he bled to death.

We hated to see those things, but it just let us know how

fragile life is. How appreciative I am, still, for each moment of each hour of each day, not knowing how long I'm going to be here, but thankful that I am, because of having seen those guys get killed.

We were instructed in our training that if a buddy were hit, try to get a medic, because our objective was to defeat the enemy, and we could not lose sight of our objective. Likewise, we could not take a bunch of prisoners–everybody quits fighting and says "Here's a prisoner!"–we couldn't do that. We had to get others to do that and we had to go ahead with our mission. In this case, when one was severely injured, we did what we could to make him comfortable and then we tried to get a medic to go there to help him. Sometimes we called with the little squad radio that we had to send a medic, and then we'd go on. That was normal.

There was a medic with each platoon, and three platoons in each company, and then a medic in charge. That would be four medics in each company. A company is about 160 soldiers so that's a ratio of one medic for every forty soldiers. They were around someplace, and they wore white arm bands and did not carry weapons, although some of them did start to carry weapons because to some of the enemy it didn't make any difference. But theoretically they're not supposed to shoot medics. A white arm band with a red cross on it: that was a medic.

Others were killed, obviously, because I guess from start to finish we lost over sixty percent of our people.

Many of the other people killed were civilians: we might throw in a hand grenade and then we'd go inside, burst inside the room and see what was there, and sometimes it was civilians, and to see civilians, with women and children, killed, we hated that! Sometimes it doesn't show that in movies, but it does happen.

It made us sad to some extent, but if we got too sad, we'd lose our own lives. We had to stay calloused to death, to having killed those people who were not really a part of the war but who were victims of the war.

We had a special respect for each other! We knew what each could do, we knew how fast he could run, we knew that he would protect us, as we advanced ahead in leap-frog fashion, from house to house or street to street.

We knew from where the artillery was coming or to where it was directed, so that we could direct our own artillery towards that direction to eliminate the enemy and all their weapons.

Even many of the churches, with magnificent church steeples and stained glass, became piles of rubble. I don't think there was a church steeple in Europe that didn't have a lot of artillery holes or bullet holes, because that was a high vantage point for the enemy to use. So as we would see them, we would direct for either the fighter planes to strafe them or artillery to shell them. Even riflemen worked on them; otherwise, the enemy would have had the advantage all the time.

We were not permitted to have diaries or to keep enemy weapons or other items. Even so, some of our people thought, initially, they wanted to collect souvenirs, like a German Lugar or P-38 pistol, and they'd try to collect one from an enemy we'd shot, and then–sure enough–they would get shot. We'd see enemy troops we'd killed with lots of gold in their teeth. Some of our U.S. troops would pick the gold out of the teeth: they'd take their knives and knock them out, with the butts of their knives, to have the gold to sell or for souvenirs. I'm sorry, but some of our people would do that. Or take watches from the dead. War is awful!

We learned very quickly not to do that because we could lose as many troops after the battle was over as during the battle, trying to get souvenirs.

Other troops had a place to put these items, a place to store them. Paratroopers had to carry and run with everything we had. We didn't have anything that was extra! We didn't do that type of thing anyway, because we were behind the enemy lines much of the time and if we had ever been caught with souvenirs, we were dead for sure. That's just all there was to it.

Even our dog tags did not have our home town on it or names of people in our family, because that could be information they could use to blackmail or sabotage some of our family. It had whether we were Protestant or Catholic or Jewish, on the dog tag, and our name and serial number. When we had one of our troops get killed, we took one dog tag and put it in his mouth, and maybe stuck the rifle in the ground with the bayonet on it, to identify where he was.

We did not ever bury any of our troops; this was for Grave Registration people. To see our own buddies killed or blown apart into pieces was demoralizing, so our leaders tried every way possible to keep us from looking at them, to keep us pushing forward. That's why we became calloused to death: we had a job to do and our job wasn't finished until the war was over.

Killer Instinct

We were well-trained troops for battle. We really were. And we had all the equipment that we needed to do the job which we were assigned, maybe not at the right place at the right time always, but at least if we ran out of ammunition we could always pick it up from a fallen buddy. We could always take his first-aid kit or, if we were out of water, his canteen in order to keep on going.

We had to be mean! Having left high school as a student, I became trained as a killer. I was a trained killer! I had to kill or be killed: it was just that simple. War is awful, and that's not normal for human beings to be that way, but we were mean and wicked.

We had been living with each other for several months, both training in the States and training overseas, and when some of our buddies would get killed or dismembered, when we saw German troops kill some of our own, then we were intent upon getting even, pushing forward.

War: we take the cream of nations' youth and put them on the battlefield killing each other, and some of those people killed are somebody's sweetheart, somebody's husband, great people for their nations. But the freedom in America was threatened so we couldn't let ourselves think, "Gosh, some of those people I killed might have been just like us, and have wives and sweethearts and parents waiting at home for them." That might have been true but we couldn't think in those terms.

And their philosophy and idea about life was quite different than ours. They were so hoodwinked with the Nazi philosophy of having a super race and doing away with everybody else. That did not set well with us; that was not what we were fighting for. We were fighting to preserve our freedom.

Because I became calloused then, perhaps I'm that way today, to injury or death. If I had been so sad or demoralized from it in the war, I would have been too weak to do the job I was assigned to do.

War is seven days a week, twenty-four hours a day. There's no eight-to-five; it's continuous. Even at night, supposedly the town is taken and the battle is over, but that doesn't mean we could rest on our laurels. We had to send out troops, every night, every night, in patrols, and they would go out and "feel out": see where the enemy was, see what the roads were, see what they had there–tanks or trucks or troops.

When we went out to search for information at night, sometimes we had little wires with a handle on each end, about three feet long, much like a starter rope on a lawn mower. As we'd go through patrols, at night, rather than shoot and give our whole position away and awaken enemy troops, we might sneak up, take this weapon and put it around the neck of an enemy soldier on patrol or who had come by us patrolling. We'd put it around his neck and pull both ends and decapitate him. War is horrible, but that's what we had to do.

With that or with a knife.

We could tell by the sound of the hobnails in the Germans' boots, the sound of a truck, the sound of a tank, the sound of automatic weapons, whether it was ours or whether it was theirs.

And, frankly, we were never really certain when we would go on patrol as to the safety of our own troops once we returned. We did have challenge words, and after D-Day each night we would change them.

We killed very few troops that we took prisoner, very few, because we wanted information from the prisoner. "Who? Where? What? Type of outfit? How many tanks are there? How many trucks? What type of unit?"

I didn't keep track of the number of people I killed, but I suspect it would be somewhere between fifty and a hundred. My uncle had taught me to shoot; he was quite a quail hunter and bird dog fancier, and he taught me how to hunt and how to aggressively go to where the quail couldn't see us as we might go around to a valley or hillside, or the backside of trees. The same type of training helped me on the front there in the war because in the Normandy area there were lots of trees and lots of hedgerows. If we'd stand on the backside of the hedgerow and look up, many of those hedgerows were six feet high or so, because all of the little plots of land around them had been farmed so long, the hedgerows were in burrows or hills around each field. So we stayed on the backside.

We had to be very careful! We listened! Our eyes and our ears were what kept us alive!

Normandy

From the 6th of June until about the 1st of August, 1944, we were there on the battlefield in the Normandy area, to give our troops a chance to get all the stuff ashore and to keep any more Germans than were already there from coming down to the beaches.

On the D-Day jump we carried everything we'd need to do our job. We couldn't carry it around, but at least we could get it to the ground. We stashed it, once we landed, in a fence row or close to a bridge location.

The regular infantry groups had their own kitchens and vehicles with them and, theoretically, they would be organized through the chain and channels of command and would know where the food stuffs were. But in the case of paratroopers, we had no kitchen or cook! They didn't jump with us! In Normandy we never ate in a camp kitchen. They dropped K-rations. I suppose it was like a picnic every day!

We jumped with three K-rations and two chocolate bars that had been issued to us. A K-ration was like a box of Cracker Jacks, in size, but wax covered so if it got wet it didn't deteriorate the food. One might have ham and eggs in a little can, potted meat or Vienna sausage. Another might have potato salad or a fruit cake. There was a package of sugar and a package of coffee. A dried fruit bar.

K-rations were made in and shipped from the United States. The other troops, coming by ship and by vehicles on the land, had C-rations, larger cans about two or three inches tall, two inches in diameter: cans of beans, fruit cocktail, pudding. We didn't have those because they were too bulky for us. Later on, the main troops had another ration that would feed a ten-man squad and came in regular sizes of food.

As far as water, we had a canteen that we jumped with. We could dip our canteen in a canal or creek, drop a couple of halizone tablets in there, shake it up, let it set for   half an hour, and then we could drink it.

The first day I could not eat at all because of seeing all the death and destruction. They didn't show this in training films, that this would happen to us! The second day I ate some K-rations.

Soon, I was able to sit on a corpse just to keep from sitting in the mud or water. I might eat my K-ration of food, the little can, or drink some water from the dead man's canteen. It was just that simple: we quickly became calloused to death, not only from seeing our own soldiers killed but also the death of German soldiers and even French civilians, and animals–cows and horses killed with the bombs and artillery shells.

We supplemented the K-rations any way we could or wanted to, until we got vehicles or kitchens. We had to rely on other types of food.

The people, not in their homes, were either killed or had gone to safer positions, but in and around their homes we had access to gardens and home-canned food. This was before the days of freezers and locker plants, and the native people would cook meat, can it, and pour lard over it in a fruit jar. We would open one of these jars, scrape the lard off, and eat some of the beef or pork that was inside. The same was true with vegetables, whether it was beans or corn or potatoes that they also had canned.

Every one of the homes had a large wood barrel on its side with cider, from many apples they had around there. There might be a hand-dug well that was right beside the barn but we'd see where they'd cleaned the barn, thrown the manure out the window, right into the well!

Because of my early upbringing on the farm, I could make do. It was amazing what we lived with, and we certainly didn't think in terms of, "Well, it's 5 o'clock, time to eat!"

Once we had our mission accomplished, then we formed a battle line so no more enemy could come down to the beaches. We were more or less stationary, we had already taken the towns, the bridges, the roads, and we could always bring in food from the rear, at that point, and from the equipment chutes that had dropped large containers.

Our main chute was a 28-foot camouflage nylon; our reserve chute, on the front, was a 24-foot white nylon; the rayon chute for the equipment was about a 32-foot, with tapes of nylon string, heavier, rather than parachute cord.

The rayon equipment chutes were different colors, maybe red, yellow, or green. The color represented whether the container was ammunition or food or medical. They were usually fastened to and carried under the belly of the plane, and could be released at any time by the cockpit.

We had what was called pack howitzer, about a 75 millimeter howitzer with which to fight artillery, that was dropped in pieces and then we assembled it quickly. Paratroop units, generally, are rapid firing, rapid moving, light equipped; we had automatic weapons, lots of hand grenades, more so than a typical infantry unit.

But a typical infantry unit would have its own trucks, and then the armor would have all of their half tracks and other vehicles in which they could haul men and equipment. We didn't have any of those! As a paratrooper jumping, we had no vehicles and no heavy artillery.

At one point, during an equipment drop, they even sent along some paint. I didn't do it, but some of the Service Company people would paint some of the captured vehicles with our army colors, a dark olive green with a white star.

All of our vehicles and tanks had a white star, about two feet in diameter from point to point, on the hood of the truck, on the top of the tank, as well as on the side. That way from the air or from the ground, the white star would let everyone know this was our own equipment because the Germans had a black and white cross on their tanks and on their trucks.

Otherwise, we might be destroyed by "friendly fire" and, unfortunately, this does happen in war time. That's how my brother, Roland, was killed.

This could have happened to me one time in Normandy. We had captured a little amphibious jeep. It was shaped more like a bathtub than one of our amphibious jeeps. We started to cross a river in it and before we got across, the Germans opened up machine gun fire on us, because they could see our uniforms were different. We hadn't had a chance to paint the jeep, it was only a means to get across the river, so we jumped out of the thing, got to shore swimming in this river, and hid on the shore until we got others to get a bead on the Germans and eliminate them. We didn't use an unpainted vehicle any more!

Of course the enemy confiscated some of our equipment chutes, in addition to other tactics to try and stop the D-Day invasion.

For example, another type of Rommel's Asparagus was supposed to prevent tanks or ships from even coming ashore. They were just as heavy as railroad tracks, made of steel and iron, with points on them. If a ship came when the tide was in, then these objects would puncture the ship or hang it up and it couldn't go any further. There were many of those along the beaches and we could see them when the tide was out.

To try and trap our tanks, every so often there would be rows of concrete barriers. Much like rows of corn, they'd be staggered one row behind the other so we couldn't get a tank through. And there would be steep ditches with water in them so we might get tanks stuck.

Our Thompson automatic weapons which a number of our troops had were a fine weapon, but they weren't made for all the sand and dirt and water, and they would get jammed up. And they were more expensive. So in order to equip our troops with more automatic weapons at a lesser price, they made what they called a Grease Gun, a little .45 caliber automatic weapon that was made out of metal, no fancy wood stock, no more than two feet long altogether. It had a different sound, but it gave us an automatic weapon that didn't jam so much as the Thompson sub-machine gun.

Sometimes in the fighting, some battles were more fierce than others. It depended on the type of troops we were fighting. The German SS, the most fierce and best trained, wore black uniforms with SS on them; they were Hitler's own elite group, dead-set that the Nazi way was the only way, and would fight to the death rather than give up. The paratroopers, the next most fierce, were very well trained, very experienced, what we called seasoned troops. The Wehrmacht, the regular army, were the ones we preferred to fight; they were the conscriptees.

When Germany took over France and Holland and Alsace Loraine and Belgium and Poland, they would take these nations' young people and put them in the German army. They called them conscriptees and forced them to fight in the German army. Not in positions of leadership, of course.

These troops in their outfit, in their units, would fight only because they had to. They might even be firing in the air, high enough where it wouldn't hit us, because they didn't really want to kill us, they wanted freedom themselves. Because they had been forced into the military, it was easier for us to take these people prisoners. As a matter of fact, they probably were very happy to be taken prisoners, because they wouldn't have to fight anymore.

So we learned very quickly–as seasoned troops *we* became–what to do, how to do it, and who we were fighting.

We learned the very sound of a weapon. Most of us would never pick up a German weapon and fire it, because our own troops would shoot in our direction! But there still was "friendly fire" from situations like that, and deaths.

And the sounds of all their weapons! Many of their paratroopers had little automatic weapons that we called their Burp Guns, because they fired so fast, they'd go "burp, burp." There might be ten rounds fired just that quickly.

We learned the sounds of airplanes, empty or bomb-laden, whether they were German planes or British planes or American planes, going or coming. And though we paratroops didn't have any trucks, our ground troops did, and we could tell which trucks were Germans and which were ours.

Many of the towns' and villages' streets were cobblestone streets, and because the Germans had hobnails in their boots, we could tell from the sounds of the boots whether they were our troops or whether they were enemy troops walking, as we'd go from house to house or street to street.

We didn't automatically shoot a prisoner. We were tempted to sometimes, because when he's firing and kills one of our buddies and then we're able to take the German prisoner, the natural desire is to kill him too. But if we shot him in front of other German troops where they might be able to see us, with field glasses or otherwise, they'd all fight 'til death, they wouldn't give up. So we learned very quickly not to kill them visibly to their own troops. We would take them back to the rear area if we were going to kill them and then do it.

Band of Brothers is a movie, based on a book. The story is from one of the paratroop units from WWII. There's nothing that can depict the actual battle lines, the battle field, because there are no cameras on the front line. Real battle is not shooting a scene, then going back and saying, "Let's rearrange it this way"! There is no "Let's shoot the movie and then we'll go rest tonight." But, I think they did the film well. By being able to see all of those things which they depicted, it came as close as could be to being the real thing.

In *Band of Brothers* there is much death and destruction: of buildings, of homes, of relationships. It shows what for us was real: young man to young man developing a special camaraderie that all of a sudden was gone. In its place were the pieces and parts of bodies and buildings lying everywhere. It shows how bad war really is.

A number of times I was lonely when I was on the battle-field front and in our fox hole and it was a quiet night. I'd look up and see the stars. I didn't forget a prayer, I can tell you that. It certainly made me think...not so much for myself but...Lord, I hope that this is over soon, and thank you for protecting me but thank you for protecting those at home. I was thinking about others much of the time: may we all get through this. We didn't really think that we were going to get killed. We wanted to think on the positive side: I want to get this war over and I'm going to do my best to advance and go to the next house or up the next street or whatever.

But several times in Normandy I thought I'd had it. One time was when we were running through someone's yard in order to reach and cross a large, open field while it was dark. As I was running across this back yard, I hit something and it knocked me immediately on my back and I thought, God, I'm dead! But I'd hit a clothes line, it had hooked on my helmet, threw my helmet back, which of course was strapped on, and I lit flat on my back.

Another time we were going across a plowed field, and the machine gun fire was coming so thick, it was just ripping holes in the Musette bag on my back, we were just that close to this machine gun. We just "swam" in the furrow of this plowed ground, so that we'd be below those bullets. We didn't know but that any minute one would get us, but thank goodness it didn't.

After the Normandy campaign–we were in battle sixty days in the Normandy area so that there could be a build-up, unloading, and stockpiling of troops and equipment, tanks, gas, supplies–we pushed out from the beachheads on across France. Heavier equipped infantry divisions and armored divisions replaced us on a line we called the St. Lo Breakthrough. This was the boundary of our lines and our troops, as opposed to the German troops, at St. Lo. They pushed forward and went across France really fast with the armor and all. They had the enemy scattered with no defense line between the Normandy area and way on in to France, until they got to the Maginot Line and Siegfried Line.

Incidentally, though I was not at St. Lo, our troops used canisters of orange smoke, to identify our own lines from the German lines, so the bombers could bomb the German lines and then our troops could push out. Well, unfortunately another "one of those things" happened, because "War is Hell" and things happen that are not planned: the wind changed and blew some of the smoke over our own troops and we bombed our own troops, too, besides the German troops! That didn't work quite as well as planned. But that's the hazards of war: there are mistakes that happen and we learned from those mistakes.

Of course, Patton and all of his armored troops, they went across France like Grant through Richmond! Fast!

We didn't have a bath when the day was over. Matter of fact, we didn't have a bath until we got R and R, Rest and Relaxation, maybe sixty days down the line! We didn't have a bath on the battlefront ever; the only "bath" we might have had was when we crossed a river or canal, or when it rained.

Enlisting

My identical twin brother, Roland Manley, had enlisted in the airborne troops because it paid more money. The troops in those days got $21 a month. That's for a private going into military service. And I looked the services over as he did.

If someone joined the Navy, it was thirteen buttons on the front of his pants. If he had to relieve himself in a hurry...well, that was not for me!

Then there were the Marines. They didn't have hip pockets in their pants and we were used to pockets all over our pants.

Well, then there were the Paratroopers! I could jump out of an airplane with a parachute! How exciting that would be! And their uniform–why, it had pockets all over! And it paid $50 more a month.

I could have joined the submarines in the Navy and be paid extra money, more than paratroopers were paid, but I didn't want anything that dangerous.

So I joined the Paratroopers because I could get $50 more a month. And then if I volunteered to go overseas, I got twenty percent more. And if I were combat infantry, then I'd get an additional ten percent or so.

Gosh! It made me feel like an executive with money coming in like that! There hadn't been much pay during and before the Depression years.

Japan's December 7, 1941 attack on Pearl Harbor was unforeseen; we were truly unsuspecting. I think time will say we had too many ships in one place. But that polarized our people in America! We said, "Hey! We're going to have to protect ourselves or we're going to be doomed to war and the threat of enemy takeover. So let's get with it!" And we did!

Everything was going to the military, and rationing was started. We wanted to take part, to protect the freedoms of America. The thing for a young man-and a young woman- to do was to go to the military service! I joined the service in the fall of 1942, my senior year, and therefore did not go through the graduation ceremonies. Many of us went into the service.

Actually, when Hitler and the Nazi Regime started war in the late 1930s and took over a number of countries, such as France, Poland, Holland, and Belgium, we saw the threat and we began getting ready. We knew that they could bring that death and destruction to us. So as our people went to the production facilities, what an opportunity that gave us to come out of the Depression!

Patriotism was so thick at that time. It's never been as great before or since as it was during those war years. We had the greatest production facilities the world has ever known! We could produce thousands and thousands of planes, thousands of trucks, thousands of tanks, thousands of guns, ammunition, artillery, all these things that are necessary to fight a war. We were able to produce very quickly, and England held off the Nazi Regime, and we held off Japan from coming onto the shores of America until we could get those production facilities in force and in place, which we did.

We even helped England and Russia with critical war needs, so they could fight and contain the enemy until we could get ready. And then when we did get ready, several years later, it came time for the start of D-Day: June 6, 1944. That was the culmination of all these years of preparation for war, all these years of producing.

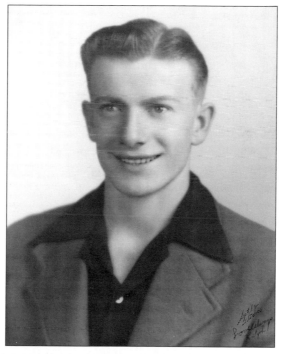

"I joined the service in the fall of 1942, my senior year. I did not go through the graduation ceremonies or anything like that. The thing for a young man to do was to go to the military service."

Training

My basic training took place at Camp Roberts in California, my paratroop training took place at Ft. Benning, Georgia, and my advanced infantry training took place at Camp McCall in North Carolina.

When my brother and I enlisted, he went first, about two months ahead of me. He'd had a spat with his girlfriend.

The first place I went was Jefferson Barracks, Missouri, in St. Louis, for only a few days, just to get processed. That meant they saw that I got various shots, certain health exams, and my uniform. That's where I was sworn in and from where I sent my civilian clothing back home. And it was icy and cold there, in December.

I decided I wanted to be in the paratroops, in the infantry, from the beginning. There was no waste of time. They sent me to Camp Roberts, California, for infantry training. My outfit of 501 had already started their basic training at Camp Toccoa, Georgia, and because everything had set cycles, like about a twelve-week program, and if someone missed about a week or two, he'd be behind, they sent me to Camp Roberts, at Paso Robles, about halfway between San Francisco and Los Angeles.

We rode troop trains and stayed in Pullman cars where we slept in beds that folded down at night. During the day there were chairs. We were packed like sardines and it was not pleasant.

A boxcar ahead of the Pullman had a GI kitchen set up that cooked the food. There were no seats in the kitchen car, but at least we got food. We had to go through the line just right so the cook could tap the spoon on the edge and the food would drop off into our mess kit that we carried.

Then there was a certain way we had to wash the mess kit, after we finished eating. They had two barrels of water: one had disinfectant and water, and the other just had rinse water. We dipped our mess kit into one barrel and rinsed it all out, then dipped it in the other barrel. Sometimes if a soldier didn't get his clean, he'd have what was called the "GI's", which meant he had a problem with his bowels. That was part of military life.

There was no shortage of food there. We had to eat what they had, of course. The only shortage of food was in the actual battle areas or zones.

I was in California twelve to sixteen weeks for infantry training on the use of the weapons: how to disassemble them, how to use the bayonet, how to attack, what to do under machine gun fire, how to use hand grenades, how to use the rifles. Not mortar training. That would be additional training at another time.

We had to do guard duty at night, in California, which they taught us. At that time Japan was an enemy, and being on the coast in the dark I remember imagining, "Gosh, I hope they don't attack the coast tonight while I'm on duty!"

In some areas, closer to the coast, they had a lot of barrage balloons, balloons that looked like dirigibles or little submarines, which had cables hanging down so low-flying planes that came in would get all tangled and wreck. They had those particularly around the shipyards in

"They sent me to Camp Roberts, California, for infantry training, Basic Training, in January, 1943."

San Francisco.

Some of the fellows either had a car there or access to a car, and by pooling rationing stamps, they were able to get enough gas and maybe even get an extra five-gallon can of gas–we called those Jerry Cans–and go to L.A. We went to L.A. in one trip, one pass, with three or four other fellows.

Then just as soon as I finished infantry training, they sent me to Fort Benning, Georgia, for parachute training, about five days and four nights on a train again. We passed through Nebraska, and it was like a bit of home! The women met the troop train, as it stopped for whatever reason, and gave us birthday cake. There might have been three or four cakes on the train, on this car.

After parachute school at Fort Benning, we had the opportunity to choose certain schools, such as demolition and espionage school or communications and radio. Otherwise, we were sent on to some parachute outfit for advanced training. I chose demolition espionage, because some of my buddies there, that I'd made friends with, chose that also.

Then they shipped me on to Camp McCall, North Carolina, a little temporary camp with one-story shacks with tar paper on the outside. That was where the 501st had their training and when I joined the parachute infantry. After training they assigned me to a regiment that was building up to its prescribed number of people.

Primarily it was full. The cadre were usually older people who had already been in other outfits or training. I went in as a private and I stayed a private until after D-Day, because there was no chance for any higher rank. We were always over our Table of Organization as far as how many we were supposed to have in each rank: only so many sergeants, so many privates, so many corporals, so many master sergeants, tech sergeants, staff sergeants. At that time, if someone wanted to transfer in to paratroops, he could keep the rank he had. So, having their cadre already by the time I got there, there was no chance to get advancement there, then.

At Camp McCall, we learned advanced training and "togetherness." And we learned about mortars.

A mortar is a large tube that has shells dropped in the top of it, and when the shell slides down and hits the bottom, it explodes like a bullet and shoots out. It almost goes straight up. Artillery shells, for example, go a long way, like a rifle bullet, but a mortar shell goes up and then down. When it explodes, when it hits, pieces of its shell go everywhere.

A mortar shell is the most dreaded military weapon because of these pieces, called shrapnel. It can even go up and come down in a foxhole with a soldier! With a bullet, he can get in a ditch and it goes over the top of him; a mortar shell, no! We learned immediately: avoid being under a tree when they're firing artillery or mortars, because when that artillery shell would hit a limb on the tree, it would explode right there; they called it a tree burst. If a mortar shell would explode there, shrapnel would come down on us.

At Camp McCall, we had maneuvers over large areas. One was a maneuver around Murfreesboro, Tennessee. We joined with the 101st Airborne as a division exercise. It was like the Red Team against the Blue Team, make-believe war. We'd advance and take over little villages that the army had bought so that they could have maneuvers. Not only did the 501 or the 101st Airborne have them here, other divisions could use it as well. Maybe one would have it for two weeks, then another would have it, then another. It was very helpful in teaching us how to work together and for practice.

We scrounged for food, too. Some of the fellows went visiting to a chicken house, and they killed some chickens, and we had to pay dear for that: we weren't supposed to do that on maneuvers!

I didn't do it, because, actually, I was a very good soldier. I did not drink; I didn't smoke; I didn't run around. I didn't gamble. But some did.

I was at Camp McCall from about July until about December of 1943. After Tennessee maneuvers, we got a week's pass to go home, and then back to camp and overseas. We were scheduled to go overseas. They didn't tell us that, but we knew. I went home to see my mother, and Grandmother at the farm, for about a week, after Camp McCall.

"In December, 1943, I went home to see my mother [Helen I. Manley] for about a week, after Camp McCall. I was on leave before going overseas with 501st Parachute Infantry Regiment, 101st Airborne Division."

"My sister [Dorothy F. Manley] was in the military service too, the Women's Army Corps (WACs) in the Air Force."

I didn't know about my brother's death until I got to Camp McCall. He had been sent to Africa, and he went from Africa with the 82nd Airborne Division to jump into Sicily, and that's where our own Navy shot down our planes as they went over the Mediterranean. That was when they gave me the chance to come home, but I was even more propelled to "go get 'em!"

My mother got a telegram about my brother's death; whether it was delivered to her by a military man, I don't know, but she got a telegram. It hurt her quite a bit; there's no doubt about it. He was among the first in Springfield who was killed in action. And she changed one of three blue stars (which represented my brother, my sister, and me) in the window flag to a gold star.

There are all kinds of mistakes like "friendly fire" in war time! Because of mistakes like that, the army came up with the Mae West life preserver, a first aid kit with morphine in it, and painting the black and white stripes around the planes. We never again lost a plane to friendly fire. All the six thousand ships in the English Channel and we never lost a plane, because now they were readily identified. Yes, we learned from our mistakes.

From Camp McCall-this was about December of '43-they put us on trains and shipped us to Boston. There they processed us at camps, with names like Miles Standish and Camp Twenty Grand, by getting the right equipment, the right shots, and the right clothing to the right troops. We left in December from Boston for England on our troop's designated ship.

Before the D-Day jump, I had five jumps from a plane and, at Fort Benning, I had numerous jumps from towers, 250 foot towers with a large ring around each one.

A tower had four arms on it, but they could never use all four because of the wind direction; we had to be away from the wind. They would draw this cable and ring way up-the parachute was open now and hooked around this ring-and

then they would press release and the parachute would float
down. We didn't have to open it up and there was no static
line. That was before the five times we actually jumped from
the plane.

The first time they taught us how to pack our own parachute. Some were so nervous they got up at midnight and
went back out, saying: "I want to know if I did this right!" Just
so worried over it! This was under the supervision of a rigger,
a person who is qualified to pack parachutes, so we knew
exactly what happened and how and so on, and everything
was just right. Then after that, the riggers did it for us, and we
never packed our chute again, unless someone just felt like he
wanted to or had to. And there might have been a few isolat-
ed cases where someone packed his two or three times, but
the vast majority of them did not.

We got $21 a month plus $50 more for parachute pay.
Then they raised the pay to $35 a month. We could have some
taken out and sent home. I purchased some additional insurance at Fort Benning, worth another $10,000, and that insur-
ance premium would come out of my pay monthly and be
sent to the insurance company. Thank goodness I never used
it! I imagine that company went broke! The limit at that time
was $10,000, what they called GI Insurance. I still have it, it's
worth about double, and the dividends from it more than pay
for the premium.

The entire year after I enlisted was training-infantry training, parachute training, and demolition training-and then putting it all into practice with a unit, the 501st Parachute
Infantry.

When I started I hardly knew the difference between a
division or a Screaming Eagle or a pot of gold. But I learned
everything I could about how the military was organized.

The 101st Airborne Division was part of the United States
Army.

The Division was made up of three Parachute Regiments. I was in the 501st Parachute Infantry Regiment. There also were the 502nd and the 506th Parachute Infantry Regiments.

There were glider outfits, like the 401st Glider Infantry and the 326th Glider Infantry. These troops that came in by glider had smaller units, fewer than 1500.

Then there were Artillery Units, Communication Units, Service Units, even a Band Unit. But the Band did not jump with us!

The Screaming Eagles were all of those who belonged to the 101st Airborne, because we had the patch, the division patch, on our shoulder. It was an eagle head with a brown or black background, a white face or head, and a red tongue.

Everything was triangular in the military service. A division was made up of three regiments; a regiment was made up of three battalions; a battalion was made up of three companies; a company was made up of three platoons; a platoon was made up of three squads.

Approximately, there were 1500 in a regiment; 500 in a battalion; 160 in a company, 50 in a platoon, 15 or so in a squad.

One squad might be a mortar squad and one might be a light mortar squad; they had 60 millimeter mortars and 81 millimeter mortars. One might be a rifle squad.

I started with Regimental Headquarters Company. Each battalion had what they called a Headquarters Company, and it would consist of specialists. For example, it might have been communications, it might have been demolition because there was a platoon of demolitionists, a platoon of communication specialists who might string out phones and have larger radios.

A, B, C companies made up the 1st battalion; D, E, F made up the 2nd battalion; G, H, I were the 3rd battalion.

Each platoon had one of the little radios so they could communicate with the company headquarters and also with each other. And the company would have contact with the battalion; the battalion would have contact with the division, so we could always pass on information. But we didn't use the radio carelessly or needlessly, because the enemy could use information if they were able to decipher or interpret it.

We learned all this in our early training.

"I was Private Ralph K. Manley until after D-Day."

Can you imagine this boy leaving a farm in Springfield, "Missourah," going in the military service and then, after rigorous and proper training for about twelve months, traveling to Boston, getting on a boat and sailing to England? Whoa!

What an experience: taking a Liberty Ship, built very quickly in war time, that traveled in a convoy of ships as an attempt to protect one another from the German submarines that were sinking ships almost daily. Every convoy lost some.

Because we zig-zagged in another attempt to avoid the German submarines, it took us eleven days by ship to get over to England. We landed in Scotland, actually, at the Firth of Clyde, the most emerald green water I'd ever seen. Then from there we got on buses which took us down to where we actually were billeted or had our tent city, on this lawn west of Newbury, England. Our group was not stationed at the same place, as far as our regiment: one was in what used to be a large horse stable and another was on grounds of a castle which had a large holding of land. My camp, in the tent city on the lawn of the castle, was made up of six-man tents.

Many of the air bases had Quonset huts, half-round corrugated metal. We didn't have any of that! That was almost semi-permanent; the tents, of course, were not permanent.

We went, on passes, to London and some of the larger cities. To see all the history of the kings and the queens and the nobility! But we'd also see where the Germans had bombed the homes, each night, and set fires to many, that forced the people from their homes

We'd go in the subways in London, in order to travel from place to place sightseeing, and we'd see some of these people whose homes or apartments were destroyed now living in the subways. Others lived in the subways because that was safety for them, down underground away from the bombs. But in the subways, the bunks were stacked five or six high, much like they had been on the troop ship we'd taken.

This had never happened to America in my lifetime and we

Americans determined right off: we were fighting to preserve our freedoms. The Germans were fighting to take over lands and enslave people. We were fighting because we knew after England, America would be next, because the submarines from Germany and the Nazi Army were here on the coast of America! We didn't want to lose our families and our homes.

Being in a strange country, with strange language and strange habits–even in England–it gave us soldiers a common bond.

Remember Elmer Neumann, the first one of my buddies to be killed in Normandy? He was from Minnesota, and he talked a little different, probably with a Swedish background, but he was a fine young man. I slept on the bottom bunk and he slept on the top bunk, in our six-man tent. This provided a family-type atmosphere in which we didn't get lonely.

We were in excellent physical shape, but mentally and spiritually we needed somebody with whom to talk about our shared experiences and training. We also shared packages that we'd get from home, such as cookies or aftershave, because packages and mail were great morale builders.

Remember when my brother was killed and they gave me the opportunity to come home but I wanted to stay, to "get even"? Most of us had that same reaction and attitude when our buddies, our colleagues, were killed in the Normandy campaign, especially the ones with whom we had trained.

Another great help with any problems we might have was the Red Cross who would congregate on Piccadilly Circus. A fellow might go there if he had a death in the family, or if he got what we call a "Dear John" letter from his sweetheart saying it's all over. Always consolation from them, and always donuts and coffee!

At that time, coffee was very scarce in England. They had imitation coffee called chicory and it didn't taste good at all! But the Red Cross had the Real McCoy! It drew us there every time we were on a pass, to get a donut and real coffee and hear language like we spoke at home, rather than the British or Cockney accent.

I remember some of the good times that we shared, like seeing a movie or show in camp, and the funny differences in the food. For example, we went on a pass to London and on a menu Neumann thought they had Welsh Rabbit (Welsh Rarebit); but it was not rabbit; we didn't get what we thought we'd ordered and we laughed together about this. We didn't order steaks because they didn't have them, but they did have lots of fish and "chips"–French fries. It wasn't the type of food we knew from home. We'd always take home something from the bakeries; they had beautiful bake shops that could be compared here to Panera Bread. Beautiful displays!

The food served by the military was good. It wasn't prepared like Grandmother would prepare it but at least it was good. In fact, many of us gained weight, even though we were exercising very heavily to get our bodies in good shape for combat. For example, at home when we had rice for breakfast in the morning, we put cream and sugar on it; this rice was more like Spanish rice and had sauces. Some of these meals used a lot of mutton. This was my first experience with mutton and I didn't care for it.

There was nothing on Sunday evening except a spam sandwich or jelly and bread. But we learned what to do and how to supplement, to have something different. We could take the lid off the little stove in our tent and scoot it to one side, bend a coat hanger over this hole where the lid would fit, and toast the bread or rolls that we'd bought, adding what I'll call Moonlight Requisitioned Butter from the mess hall.

This was in training in England, before we went on the D-Day invasion, living in six-man tents on a castle lawn. We were training every day, physically as well as mentally. We would study and see and drive enemy vehicles, probably captured from Africa, in order to see and hear the differences. We also learned to drive a railroad engine and a tank, and to fly an airplane, a little Piper Cub which would be like an artillery spotter.

We learned that eyes and ears were the greatest thing we could have, because this told us about the enemy. And I learned then that if I'm going to produce well, I must feel well, because we had calisthenics and physical training every day and were in top physical shape as human beings, ready to go through all the rigors that were necessary to fight a war: from running, from leaping, from doing without food, from doing without sleep at certain time periods in order to accomplish our mission.

Of course, we had infantry training and had to go through periods of crawling while machine gun fire was going over the top of us, designed to teach us to keep low. Anytime we heard machine guns, we were to get as low to the ground as we could, because we had a better survival chance. Maybe because we knew it was training and safe, some didn't remember to keep low when we were actually in battle!

Because I was young and naïve, I remember thinking: "With all the goods and services and people that are now in England, in addition to the English people, I hope this island doesn't sink!"

They taught us about the invasion money we would be issued, money printed by our government, the US Banknote Company in America, and that was what we had in France or Holland or Belgium or Germany. It was about $25 that they would issue us for each nation as we'd go in there, to try and buy information .

Well, I'm sorry to say, soldiers don't buy much information in war time; they don't buy much of anything; they take whatever they want. But there were certain civilians whom we would befriend, rather than destroy, and pay for answers to questions such as "where is the enemy? what do they have? what outfit do they belong to?"

They also issued us little books, about a three-inch-by-four-inch book of French language, as part of our equipment for going into that country. This dictionary would have an English word and then the French equivalent or vice versa. The same way with Belgium, Holland, Germany. Little books that would let us speak and converse with the people of that nation in a way that we could understand each other. Of course, hands are always a great thing, and we could point to or draw a picture of a cow if we were trying to say "where are the cows?" We could usually converse; sometimes it just took a little bit longer!

We were taught to try and get along with each other because together we could accomplish our mission. No one outfit did it; no one service did it. The Navy did their part, the Army did their part, the Air Force did their part, the Coast Guard did their part, and those at home on the production line did their part. It was togetherness that really wove us into a great nation and a great patriotic people at that time.

Stressed heavily in our training was name, rank, and serial number: if we were captured, they did not want us to give any information other than name, rank, and serial number: that's all.

We were shown sand tables, with the highway networks, the large landmarks such as church steeples, to which we could orient ourselves once we hit the ground. We were clearly told our job. I knew mine was to disrupt communications first, and by being a demolitionist, I was to blow the utility lines with explosives, then put anti-tank mines on the road leading down to the beach so that German troops could not come down, anymore than what were already there, could not reinforce any of the troops that were guarding the beaches. We were to block all the road junctions.

All this we learned in our training in England, before D-Day.

Return to England

After almost two months in Normandy, we were relieved with ground troops who had come ashore. We went back to England to get new supplies and replacements for those who were killed or wounded, and to get ready to jump again.

I was put into G Company because several of my people had gone down with our plane in Normandy and it was thought best for us to be with a company. In G Company I became responsible for communicating with the platoon by operating a little SCR radio, about three inches thick and about a foot long.

Well, they had several jumps scheduled for us, but Patton went across France so fast that by the time we'd get ready for a scheduled jump to take over a certain town, he was already there! And so they'd postpone it, postpone it, postpone it, and we didn't get to jump anymore into France.

While we waited, we wrote home, but with censorship we couldn't tell where we were or who we were or about other buddies. We couldn't even send pictures of our division patch. We had to sew our division patch on our shoulder, but when we sent the picture home they would cut the patch out! I don't know why but that was part of The Plan.

Holland

The D-Day jump into Normandy was June 6, 1944. Our next jump, the 17th of September, 1944, was into Holland. This was to preserve what I call a shoestring highway clear across France and Holland and Belgium, so General Montgomery, the British General, could move his armor on it into Germany through the back door, as opposed to hitting the front line, called the Siegfried Line, the line between France and Germany.

Before we ever got there, England had been thrown back when they tried to land in France on their own. It was a failure. Now they needed a winner, something positive, so General Montgomery was very well equipped with armor to go on these roads and bridges which we were to protect.

D-Day was a nighttime jump. Of course, the odds were against us, because the Germans were in fixed positions, all ready with their fox holes, all ready with their pill boxes, all ready with their tunnels leading from one to another, that type of thing. On any nighttime jump, we were going to lose about fifteen percent of our troops with injuries resulting from all the equipment they had to carry, from landing on roofs or church steeples, in trees, in deep water, whatever.

But the Holland jump was into big wide-open fields, not flooded, on a sunny afternoon, and we lost very few troops with injuries on the jump itself. I didn't see any enemy in the moments we landed.

They have lots of canals in Holland because it is below sea level and, as such, they have to pump water out. A daylight jump and getting well organized were certainly to our advantage. We got assembled rather easily because we were all together, and the Dutch Underground, called Orange, met us on the Drop Zone.

The Dutch Underground had radio contact with higher authorities than what we were, and told us where the Germans were, what they had, and within a few minutes we got assembled and with our bazookas–which were rocket launchers, we called them bazookas–we were able to proceed to a highway and knock out three German tanks rather quickly because we surprised them.

As a matter of fact, some of our troops even waved to them, they waved back, they didn't even know what the devil was happening! I don't think it had been fifteen minutes! The Underground had told us where they were; they were not moving at the time; they were there having lunch or something, it was mid-afternoon, about one or two o'clock.

Because our assignment was to keep the highway open, that placed us on either side of the highway, in fox holes and ditches, and protecting all the bridges so that Montgomery's British armor could get on through.

These were the three airborne divisions in the Holland jump: the American 101st Airborne Division, the American 82nd Airborne Division, and the British 1st Airborne Division.

Since this was a British idea, the British 1st Airborne Division jumped at Arnhem, Holland, a town on the banks of the Rhine River, coming in the back door to Germany. The Germans were very heavily fortified there and it was a disaster for the British 1st. They suffered severe losses, were either killed or captured. The British 1st Airborne Division included a number of Canadians, Australians, New Zealanders, Polish, French, smaller units that had been stationed in England who had fled the Germans as they took over France, and they were all organized–quite well, I might add–to jump.

The 82nd Airborne Division jumped at Nijmegen, Holland, and of course strung out all along the road, protecting the highway and the bridges, to get the armor up there in a hurry. But it was a disaster for the 82nd as well; they suffered severe losses, and I don't think there were many captured.

Then our 101st was assigned the lower end of Holland. I jumped at Veghel, Holland, a pretty much open, flat territory, not the hedgerows and very small fields that we saw in Normandy.

Again, it was to protect the highway and the bridges, and the bridges were smaller than Normandy because it was, obviously, not hilly and not a lot of timber. It was easier to take because we could see miles away at times. The highest structures were typical Dutch windmills that had the large blades on them and were used to grind the grain.

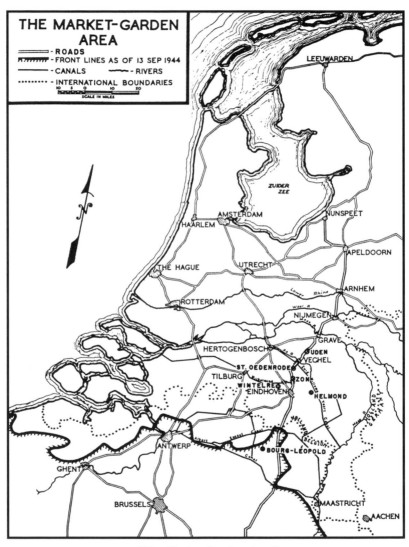

"The Market-Garden Area"
"The next jump was into Holland, which was the
17th of September, 1944."

Virgil Danforth, a soldier in our outfit, was stationed in one of these windmills to scout the long distances with his field glasses and see about where the Germans were. Though shelling knocked some of the bricks and blades off that windmill, he continued to direct our mortar fire as the Germans got closer. He received the Distinguished Service Cross for his service in that windmill at Veghel, Holland.

From Holland we went back to Mourmelon, France to wait once again for another jump. We were there about sixty days. This was a French Army Camp that the Germans had taken over. It was really archaic, compared to other known military camps, did not have the luxury of heat-which we actually didn't need at that time-but it didn't even have indoor plumbing. We had to fix up our own sun-heated showers, and it had outhouses.

The outhouses had three and four holers, and they were always on a little hill or ramp. On the back side would be large, thirty-gallon buckets with handles, and all the human waste would go in there; then they would take it out and put that on their farmland. That's why we were told: never eat anything grown there!

Soon after we got back to Mourmelon, we got a pass. They didn't have then what they now call R&R, Rest and Relaxation, but they did say, "You get a pass to Paris," because we'd been fighting quite some time and we needed a getaway. So we went to Paris.

I was not a smoker but I had a package of cigarettes with me, and I traded that package of cigarettes at one of the fancy shops in Paris for a shave, a haircut, a manicure, and a pedicure. I thought that was the biggest bargain! But they really wanted American cigarettes because cigarettes were in very short supply for the civilian population in England and France as well as other nations, though not for the American soldier.

So we were in Paris on our first R&R when the loud speakers came on and urged, "All troops report back to your base units immediately!" We had no choice but to get on buses or trains and go back to our base at Mourmelon. It was just a twenty-four hour pass and I don't suppose I was there over ten hours. Certainly not enough to spend the night!

Bastogne: The Battle of the Bulge

When we got back to the base, we were informed that the Germans had overrun many of our units and we were going to Bastogne immediately. There was not time to plan an air drop, because it happened so fast, with the German troops advancing the way that they had, up to Bastogne and even around Bastogne, but not through Bastogne. The Germans were trying to attack but they did not and could not get into Bastogne because we held them.

Bastogne was in Belgium. This was the last offensive the Germans could muster together, and it had worked well up to that point, because they had broken through our lines; that was the bulge. They had quite a bit of armor and were trying everything to win the war.

Much of our armor was with Patton's army, down in France. Once that announcement came, Patton was ordered to bring some of his armor up to that area to break through and to halt the Germans, which he did.

Even our own commanding general, General Maxwell Taylor, was in Washington at that moment to see about the plans for the 101st Airborne Division to go to Japan from Europe, since they thought the war was really over at that time. Yes, they thought it would be over in December. But it was not.

The assistant division commander, General Anthony McAuliffe, a Brigadier General, was in command, and the Germans sent some people in, three of them as I recall, with a white flag, to ask us to surrender.

Of course, our troops blindfolded them and led them to our quarters. I was not one who led them there but we were all informed of what happened.

These Germans said they would give us one hour to surrender or be annihilated. Well, that's when our own Anthony McAuliffe sent back the reply with them that was reported to be "Nuts!" But, in fact, his response was censored quite a bit after the fact! They still have his response around in a number of places, even on statues and remembrances in Bastogne.

So, because we couldn't jump, we paratroops just loaded on port battalion trucks, semi-trailer trucks with four-foot sidewalls that had been used by port battalion units to bring supplies up to the front, such as gasoline or foodstuffs or ammunition, which the troops needed on the front line. It was port battalion trucks that we rode on, from Mourmelon, France up to Bastogne.

Some of the trucks coming out on the highway before we got into Bastogne had some of the injured and dead on them. As one flung around the corner of a road, some of the body parts, a couple of arms or legs fell off the truck, and some of the troops marching, clerks or air force people or people who normally would not be combat troops but maybe service troops, when they saw that–body parts fall off the truck– some of them just keeled over, that was new to them, they just couldn't stand it.

These injured and dead troops we passed were on a "tactical withdrawal" from the front. The American Army doesn't have such a thing as retreat; they have what they call a "tactical withdrawal."

As I understand it, the 106th infantry division was a new division; they had just been put on line at Bastogne. They were not what we'd called seasoned troops, and they were hit very heavy because they did not know how to fight. They hadn't been there long enough.

To stop that, it took lots of things.

This was winter, about the 17th of December in 1944. There was about a foot of ice and snow on the ground, and about zero degrees at that time in Bastogne.

Bastogne was a road center, a road junction, and we had to use the road if we were going to move equipment, tanks, and trucks. There was lots of wooded forest around also, but it didn't work to cross the fields with snow. It didn't work for the Germans either; they had to use the roads, a hard surface.

By blocking all the roads at this road junction, of several highways coming together, then they couldn't go any further that way...on the roads. So that's what we were to do: we were in Bastogne to block all the roads.

It was dark when we got there.

Once we got into place–we had taken what ammunition we had–and we had anti-tank mines. Being demolitionists, we put anti-tank mines across all the roads going in, and had them in a fox hole alongside the roads or barn lots, wherever the road passed by.

I know where I was–near a barn lot where they had animals. Where all the feces and manure was from the animals is where the ground was not frozen as hard. So that's where I dug a foxhole, in that. I dug at the edge of a culvert and used the culvert as a place to kind of scoot in also, because there was no snow in there. But all the barnyard stuff, well, who cared about the smell?

We blocked the roads and formed a circle around Bastogne so the Germans could not go any further.

A little later, a truckload of mines and ammunition had been brought in to Bastogne, and some of my demolition group were unloading it so they could have additional supplies around the roads where they were needed, and this truck got a direct hit from German shelling, and it killed about thirteen of the demolition people there with that one blow. Today there's a monument to that event in one of their cemeteries, along the cemetery wall, and it lists all the names of those that the Belgium people have put there and honored and pay their respects to, each

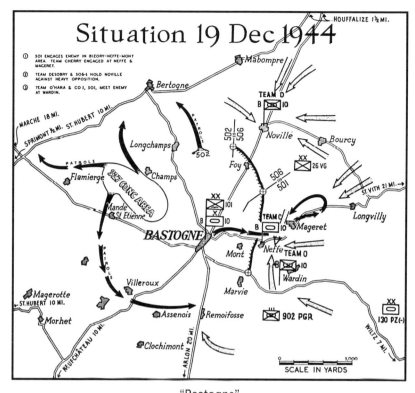

"Bastogne"
"This was winter, about the 17th of December in 1944."

Memorial Day or whatever, and have flowers there.

Paratroopers normally are a quick-headed, fast-fighting, quick-moving type of outfit with modest equipment-75 mm pack howitzers, artillery that could be dropped in two or three pieces in a chute and then assembled, on the ground. We shouldn't have been expected to fight tanks very well with those howitzers, with our hand grenades, and pistols and rifles and bazookas.

But we did! Once we disabled a tank with mines hidden on the road, then we could put explosives on the rear edge of it, blow the engine, and it couldn't move any further.

We were fighting the weather as much as the enemy. The temperature was about zero degrees, and there was still about a foot of ice and snow on the ground. Because we had left so hurriedly, we did not have the proper overshoes and overcoats. Some were even in their Class A or Dress Uniforms because they'd just come from R & R. We had not yet received replacement uniforms or additional equipment that we needed.

We had two men to a foxhole because two men could keep warmer and be safer. As one man could sleep five, ten, fifteen minutes during lulls, the other could keep watch. Then vice versa. Or as one watched, the other could take off his boots and rub his toes, because they were cold and wet from the melting snow and ice. He'd put his socks underneath his arms or between his legs to dry them some, from the body heat, then put his socks back on.

If we didn't do that, frostbite would set in. Many troops had frostbite where toes would freeze and gangrene would set in from lack of circulation. And there wasn't much treatment that could be done for that.

We didn't always have shelter during the snow and ice and rain. But sometimes we might get a torn piece of tin off a roof, or a car door, and put it over the top of the foxhole at least partway, to protect us somewhat. Incidentally, I almost never slept in a bed from the time the war started until the time it ended. We slept in foxholes, haystacks, barns, or behind a bunker or a dike.

We were on the short side as far as clothing and ammunition and troops, but at least we had the fighting experience. And we really hoped the war would be over and we could be home by Christmas. But our planes couldn't fly until the weather broke, and that wasn't until around the 26th of December. When they could, that was what broke the back of the German onslaught. The air force was able to strafe and bomb and our planes were able to fly to get supplies to us.

It was most difficult there, in Bastogne, so one of the nicest things after the planes came, after Christmas, was the mail.

Mail: that great morale booster. Imagine bringing in mail when we were surrounded! Actually, we were always surrounded and had been fighting from the 17th of December on.

At Bastogne there were times when I thought I'd had it, especially once when we were under some of the trees and artillery shells came in and broke large chunks of ice off fir trees, Christmas trees. One ice chunk hit my helmet, knocked it agog, and I thought, "Man, I've had my head blown off!" It was scary!

I still have a broken bone in my foot because I was in a second story window, trying to look out and fire into some buildings there in Bastogne, and they started shelling my building, so I jumped out the window into rubble down below, and my foot hit just a little bit wrong and broke a bone, which still bothers me on occasion. It's one bone sitting on top of the other, rather than joint to joint.

The Front at that time had been relatively quiet. Our "higher-ups" were getting ready to regroup for our final onslaught to win the war. They really thought the war was over and it was just a matter of cleaning up. They were not anticipating Bastogne's "Battle of the Bulge" and had put in one of our "green" divisions, who proceeded to be slaughtered! So they called us seasoned troops off of R&R.

When our planes came after Christmas, the German troops were pushed away and knew they were defeated. Soon after, there was really no hard fighting, and they surrendered in mass numbers.

After Bastogne, I went back to France to the hospital. I had been wounded six times, had some frostbite, some infection from some of the wounds, and needed to get some of the metal out. We were very thankful for sulfa powder and penicillin, what we called the miracle drugs, because they did help with the healing process.

From Christmas, December in Bastogne, it was still some five months away until the war ended, the 8th of May, 1945. My own outfit went down to Bavaria, to Hitler's special hideout, at Berchtesgaden. That's when we began fully discovering how the enemy-the Nazi Regime-had been fighting to take over lands and enslave people.

Someone who said anything against the leaders or against the government was put in a concentration camp. A Jew was either put to death immediately or put in a concentration camp. The concentration camps were skin and bones, starvation, and large trenches filled with hundreds of bodies at one time, run over with bulldozers to mash them down and then covered over with dirt-as we do trash at a sanitary landfill here in America.

We were reminded that we were fighting for freedom, including speaking out without the threat of being put in a concentration camp or killed.

May 8th, 1945, was V-E Day. Victory in Europe was what we all had been waiting for. Talk about the reaction at the end of the war! Of course, everybody wanted to drink. I was a teetotaler, so that was no problem for me, but sometimes I had to hold up nothing more than a canteen cup with water in it and act like I was drinking.

Any time a civilian would see an American soldier, she or he wanted to hug or let him know how appreciative everyone was that the war was over. They had been through horrible, horrible experiences! Their homes had been torn asunder, their animals killed, some of their family killed, some put in concentration camps-all of this and more.

After the war was over, I ended up back in England for a while to make certain all my wounds were healed. I wasn't in the hospital all that time. Because the fighting was over, they had this easy job as a means of keeping us busy: I was part of an outfit that was handling the switchboards for the military, with the old-fashioned telephones.

Then I came back home on a hospital ship. I remember it was a Liberty Ship, called the *Francis Slanger*; she was one of the first nurses who had been killed in the war. I think it took about six days to come back, but after the eleven days that it had taken on a troop ship to go over, six days seemed short.

Home

On the *Francis Slanger* we came back in to New York and when we saw the Statue of Liberty, it brought tears to our eyes. This was the symbol of freedom, a symbol that France gave to America as one of good friendship. We were very happy to be home, very happy. There were crowds waiting there for us.

I had been overseas almost two years–away from home, with strange people, strange languages, strange habits and strange cultures, and then all the horrible war experiences! We walked down the gangplank of that ship and just had to bend down and kiss the ground because we were so thankful to be home.

In New York, some of my buddies and I went to a café to get a glass of milk. I wanted milk! We didn't have milk overseas except at the D-Day meal, before we left for D-Day. Oh, there might have been a time when I milked a cow, squirted some milk in my mouth as I had learned to do on the farm. But, we were in this café and I was going to drink this milk, and one of my buddies said, "You don't want to drink that! It has lipstick on that glass!" I said, "I'm so happy to get milk, I don't give a damn about that lipstick!"

There were hoards of us heading from New York to various processing centers where we would be properly discharged. We didn't fly; we used trains to travel to the center closest to home that had space. For me it was Camp Carson, Colorado, and I was there about a week. Then I got a pass to come home.

They wouldn't release us until midnight so it could count as another day. But there weren't any planes or trains or buses leaving at that time in the morning. So I got a piece of cardboard from a box at that military camp and put JUST BACK OVERSEAS–SPRINGFIELD, MISSOURI. And the first truck that came along was a Fadler Produce Company truck that had a facility here in Springfield, Missouri, going to Tulsa. And the driver said, "I'll take you to Tulsa and we'll have another truck immediately going from Tulsa to Springfield," so I got that ride with that truck driver just because of that sign.

I don't think anything else, any bus, could have gotten here. That was my ride home from overseas! I talked all the time on the truck; I didn't sleep. The driver liked that!

Fadler Produce Company is no longer here in Springfield, but at that time they were the main produce company in town. I got a taxi cab, at the Fadler Produce Store in Springfield.

I went home to my mother's. She lived in town and was there when I arrived. That was the first time she had seen me in two years. She'd had all three of her children in the service. My sister arrived home before I did. Mother showed us her flag with three stars on it, in the window: two blue stars for Dorothy and me, and the gold star for Roland.

Patriotism was still running very thick on the home front because everyone had sacrificed so much. They hadn't been able to buy a number of things, such as gasoline, tires, batteries, and new vehicles, and had to go to junk yards to try and get salvage parts to fix the car. They'd put a boot in the tire, if it was cut, knowing it was unsafe but better than nothing. They'd also had rationing for many of the foodstuffs such as sugar, coffee, and syrup. There was not much clothing available, certainly no silk hose; most of the silk had come from Japan, and of course the war against Japan ended that.

We had our military clothes when we got discharged from the service, and we couldn't find new clothes to buy. My mother, somehow, bought a pair of blue pants for me, and a hat. I felt as though I had an umbrella on my head with that hat because we had an overseas cap with no brim in the military service. And I was just not at all used to pants that were blue. I couldn't wear either one of them.

Classes at the college had started in September, but neither my sister nor I was home at that time. We each enrolled in classes but couldn't start until the next semester, in January.

Our "band of brothers" had a strong understanding that "if something happens to me, would you share with those at home, my loved ones, some of the horrors and what we had to go through in order to live, up to that moment?"

So I did. It was in the spring of 1946 before I visited any of the families. I went by myself, and paid my own travel expenses. It was purely volunteer; the military hadn't encouraged or discouraged it. I visited at least a half dozen people, in their homes, whose son or husband had been killed, and shared with them about the horrors of war.

They had many questions. They wanted to know as much as they could about everyday life before the battles started, before D-Day started. What did he do, what did he say, how did he get along–all these things. What I would tell them is that we were genuinely happy, to the extent that we were with each other and we were family to each other, we were a band of brothers because it was all we had there.

I shared all the good things, as well as how he died, and it brought closure to his family. Of course they all wanted to know: did he suffer? In the case of my buddy Elmer Neumann, the first one to die at D-Day, he didn't suffer; he didn't know what hit him!

The bodies were still back in Europe or on the battlegrounds where they had fought and died. Later, we were the only nation to honor each family who requested the body be brought back from Europe where he was killed, back to America, to the hometown and home cemetery. And many families wanted this. But before the bodies could be returned, which was a while after the war ended, I would go and visit these people and tell them about our everyday life, and only the good things, the good things, because I'm a very positive person.

I had retained each of those situations, the time of day, the town, how many days we'd fought until then, as much as I could. But with no calendar, I didn't know Monday from Tuesday, or Wednesday from Thursday. I shared with them how he was a good fighter until that time, and how he might have saved my life, which he had, because we'd leap frog, so to speak, as we were going through towns, and he would cover me and fire while I'd run ahead, and I'd cover while he would run ahead.

I didn't just blurt out, "He was shot in the head and killed." That was not the way. I'd start out: "What a great buddy he was!" I'd describe how we lived together in the tent, in training. And that we called the mattresses Fart Sacks. They had straw in them, the food was so different, and that was what we called our mattresses. We laughed about this.

And because I'd shared other things with the sons, maybe the joys that we'd heard from home: "Dad is now working at the airplane factory" or "He's a machinist with such and such a shipyard," these family members were familiar. Letters I would get from home: "Bossy, she had her calf last week, a nice heifer calf. Well, we're turning this cow dry now because she's going to have a calf next month. We plowed the north forty for wheat today, or just finished it; Grandpa's going to disk tomorrow," that type of thing we'd shared. Letters from home, simple perhaps, had kept us apprised of home. "Your sister's going to go to school tomorrow"–all these things from each family was what we shared with each other. So when I visited with these families, they were familiar!

Everyone was very thankful, most thankful, because they loved their sons and husbands. As sympathetic and as understanding as I could be, I shared with them the everyday experiences of going over, of camp life, and then of battlefield life. What we trained in, how "he shaved every day, he brushed his teeth every night"–this type of thing–and that, quite frankly, when we went to battle, we didn't have a razor with us and we didn't have a toothbrush with us, we didn't even have soap with us, and the only bath we had was when we crossed the river or when it rained.

I continued writing those people for twenty years, until they passed away. Even two years ago I got a letter from Elmer's brother, asking how I was. That would have been 58 years! He's very aged now, his parents have passed away, but it was good to hear from him.

I didn't feel sad from those visits; I felt relieved. I felt closure because I shared all the happenings, finally, with those who cared.

I would imagine that other veterans did what I did, but I don't really know. I just did that on my own. I haven't talked with anybody else that had. As far as I can imagine, I think all infantry units particularly–and maybe air force units, too, I don't know–might have that same type of camaraderie or understanding: "If something happens, let my family know."

For my own brother, we requested his body be brought back from Sicily, and he was in a nice casket, all bolted down. We could get in if we wanted, but it wasn't like a typical casket where the lever is pressed and it opens the lid. It was a beautiful casket.

We found out the details of his death. The Graves Registration people were in charge.

He drowned in the Mediterranean but his body was recovered. The Navy, of course, picked up some of them, because the Navy was the one that shot them down. With all the clothes on, the clothes themselves would almost be like a flotation device. Trousers tucked into boots, it was like having a life preserver on, although they did not have one.

Roland was re-buried in Springfield's National Cemetery in 1947. I went on active duty three days to be escort for his casket and body from Kansas City to Springfield by train. The American Legion provided the Honor Guard.

"My twin brother Roland's re-burial was in Springfield's National Cemetery, after WWII, 1947. I went on active duty three days to be escort for Roland's casket and body from Kansas City to Springfield by train. The American Legion provided the Honor Guard."

There was no type of debriefing, to get from killer back to student. We should have had it. Just the memories of so much death and destruction had such an impact that I couldn't think clearly. Because the GI Bill paid for my tuition and supplies, I enrolled in Drury College, which started in January. I signed up for Geometry and Chemistry, and I failed them both! That was too much! I could hardly sit down long enough to study and, frankly, didn't even care that much. The next semester I knew better what to do and was able to adjust. After that, I did fine in school.

I mostly lived at my grandparents' when I came back from the war, because they still had the farm and needed help. They couldn't buy machinery, they couldn't buy repair parts, they still had the cattle to milk, the dairy, they needed some fences built. Grandpa was dead. My uncle ran the farm.

I wasn't ready to settle down. I guess I wanted peace and quiet and jobs to take my mind off the war. The farm did that pretty much. College didn't. And I'd see other young people...I wasn't about to join a fraternity because to go through hazing to join a fraternity, no way! I was a man by then! I didn't really fit with those students, but as other veterans enrolled, then I had something in common with some other students.

I felt guilty for killing people, because the people I killed were sons and husbands of families also. As I reflected, here I'd come home to my family and they couldn't, because I killed them. It bothered me some, and I needed a certain type of counseling which I didn't get. There were too many of us; it just didn't work.

And not only did I feel guilty, but, Ralph Manley wouldn't hurt a fly! I wasn't really a killer! I had to make a transition back, from a killer to a student and to who I really was, and it took a while to do that.

As a matter of fact, it took me about ten years to be able to sleep soundly at night. Every little wind blowing a limb or a leaf, or rattling against a screen, would keep me awake and ready to be alert. I'd have to check and make sure everything was all right before I could go back to sleep.

I was almost 23 when I started college. I'm in perfect health today at 82 years of age, except for that bone in my foot. And my hearing is not so good, partly because of the war.

Part 2

COLLEGE,
SUCCESS IN BUSINESS,
AND PUBLIC SERVICE

The war: that's what made me who I am today! Being a paratrooper was risky. Being a businessman has also been risky. But it will be the risk takers who will keep America going great in future generations. In fact, risk takers make the world go 'round!

The GI Bill and College

I went to college on the GI Bill. The people who stayed home and worked, sacrificed and went through rationing, they paid for my education with their taxes. By going to college I was able to get an education and put the odds in my favor.

I'm very thankful for some of the professors I had in Drury College as I was going through to get a bachelor's degree in economics. One was Dr. Meador, a local man and a professor there for many years. While he was almost blind, he was a great instructor and taught me the basics of management, of the economic system.

Dr. Wilber Bothwell, a former military man, was a lawyer who came back to college to teach as I started college, and he taught me the basics which I have always used. For example, have a good understanding of people and be able to write and communicate. With skills like these, I have been able to get other people to help me do what I wanted done, which was to leverage my time and my money to do far more than what I could do by myself.

I learned from one of the professors who taught a class in swimming before they had built a swimming pool yet at the college. He said he would teach his students how to dive, how to swim, how to use their arms, how to use their feet, but when they got the pool finished and he took the swimming class to the swimming pool, there wasn't a one of them could swim worth a darn. He said, "If you're going to learn to swim, you have to get in the water."

I decided right then and there: if I was going to learn business, I'd better get in to a business. If I was going to get in to a business, I'd better know how that business operates. And if I was going to know how it operates, I'd better understand it's not just production. There's finance; there's employees; there's suppliers. And I would have nothing unless I could sell what I produced to customers. A business is dependent upon other people.

In college I learned that my chance for success was nil unless I learned to work with others. And I learned very early in college that we need good managers because so many people are poor managers of their time and their money.

Building First Home

When I returned home, after the military service, I wanted to have my own home rather than live with my mother or with my grandparents again. I was twenty-one years of age and felt that I was a man.

I decided to build a little home. I didn't physically receive much of my pay when I was in the army; on the battlefront there's no paymaster! So when I was discharged from the military service in the late fall of 1945, I received a large paycheck. With some of it I bought a lot in town, in Springfield, on the corner of Sunshine and Fort Streets. Gosh, it cost $750 for that lot! I also had enough from my war-time wages to pay for much of the materials to build that first house.

I had learned to build by living on a farm. My grandfather and my uncle taught me how to use tools to measure, to saw, to plumb, among the other necessary skills. I helped them build the stanchions for the cattle, the corral pens, and the outhouse, for example.

So I bought that lot and since I already knew how to patch, repair, and build with tools, I built a little house. There's an Avis Car Rental Agency at that location now.

Materials were very hard to get at that time. Rationing was still on because the production lines had not changed from military or war-time production back to peace-time production. We used a lot of yellow lumber, which was made in Arkansas from small pine trees, but we didn't want the sun to shine on it very long because that would make it warp, curl up so badly. But at least it was better than nothing, because it took a long time for supply lines to get back to the civilian needs.

I used whatever windows I could get, oddballs that maybe

were old but still useable, or some that were salvage and had been taken out before an old house was destroyed. The floor was concrete and the walls were framed mostly out of the yellow pine. I hauled brick from a brick sidewalk that had been taken up and replaced with a concrete sidewalk. I was never a bricklayer, but I laid that brick! That taught me how I could do new things.

At the time, in 1946, there were no two- and three-car garages. A single-car garage, two bedrooms, and a single bath was the most popular home and was the cheapest to build. There was no air-conditioning, and the heating was through the floor, a gas furnace. I called them a kid toaster, because if a kid fell on one of the vents, it really toasted him, he'd look like a waffle! But it was better than a wood stove.

Selling First Home

I managed to build that small home and before I had it finished, some person wanted to buy it for $5,000, which would give me a profit of $1500. I knew that was not a bad deal! I sold it and said, "Well, I'll build another."

I quickly discovered they were easy to sell. A veteran could get what was called a GI Loan or VA Loan, 100% financing, no required down-payment, so it was easy to sell homes and other items.

That second one also sold for a profit, so I built a third. All the time I was going through college I was building houses, mostly by myself.

Then Grandmother Kreider gave me a little five-acre tract, off the corner of one tract of her farm, which was across the street from her home, so I might build a house when I married my wife in 1950 after college. We built that home, which is still standing, by the way.

When somebody wanted the house I was living in, rather than the one I was building or had just built to sell, then I would move from one to another. And I sold that house across the street from Grandmother Kreider for $19,000, which was a very good price at the time. Incidentally, I bought that home back two years ago for $75,000, that same house, and I refurbished it and sold it for $95,000.

Leveraging in Construction Business

I enjoyed the building, and later I enjoyed the teaching, but when I set goals I said, "Gee, I'd like to have $100,000." When I went to college, on the GI Bill after the war, the professors made only $3600 to $4200 a year salary, so I knew teaching alone would not allow me to reach my goals.

Later, I wanted $500,000 so I could have money with which to build, and eventually, I wanted to have a million dollars to have even more opportunities to buy and develop land. I knew that a house on a lot started with a large piece of land developed into lots.

By myself I could build about three or four houses a year. But if I took my skill and my money and leveraged them, then I could build six, eight, ten houses a year. By getting other people to help me with what I wanted done, when I wanted it done, how I wanted it done, for the price that I was willing to pay, I could leverage my skill and my money.

I didn't have to know how to do everything; I could hire a skilled bricklayer, plumber, electrician, or paper hanger and that way I could build more houses per year. That's leveraging.

As far as help on construction, it was just a year after I started that I hired someone else. Just a year! I did not hire a relative first, but an old-time carpenter by the name of Williams because he had the skills to cut rafters and to make what is called a hip roof, a popular roof that doesn't have a high gable and therefore is easier to paint.

Williams taught me that, as well as a lot more about building. With his help on rafters we were able to build and alternate homes next to each other, a gable roof and then a hip roof, design the entire development so they didn't look so close together. Houses six feet apart shouldn't both have gable roofs.

We tried to get a roof on the house as quickly as possible so when the weather was rainy or bad, we could have inside work like putting in the wiring or the plumbing or the insulation or the sheet rock.

Many of them we plastered, in those days. We'd put on the plaster board and then the plasterer would cover it with a mixture of sand, plaster, water, and stucco. It went on in two coats: one in a rough coat and the next one a white finish coat, much like the walls in this office today except this is dry wall or sheet rock.

After we got that done, we'd run the furnace to dry everything out because there were tons of water in the house in the wet plaster. We could build the door frames, jams, other inside things while the plaster was drying. We'd try to get the single-car garage finished, too.

Of course, in those days everything was not all brick but cheaper wood siding, as it became available, and wood windows which we had to paint ourselves.

We structured the whole process to please the buyer. And that's true today: we listen to the buyer, we please the buyer. He's not only the one who buys the product, he's the one who enables us to recover the cost of producing the product as well as make a profit.

I believe I've been successful in my business because I've been able to use other people and other people's money to fulfill my dreams and goals. The banker who was lending me other people's money wanted it back with interest. If I could pay him back when and how it was due, he could trust me and then I could borrow even more. But unless I had faith and confidence in myself, I could not have done it.

I tell others: have faith in yourself; trust, believe in, encourage, help, and teach other people; together you can accomplish many, many things. In my case, it was homes for people who need and want homes.

So from building two, three, four houses a year at first, I built 100 homes in my biggest year, ranging in price from $80,000 to $150,000 each.

As this became an empire–because that's what it's been for me–I was able to have about seventy-five different craftspeople work on a house, with their various trades and skills, from the time a house was started until it was finished. I didn't have to know it all!

They needed me, too. Many craftspeople are not sales people; they're not people with good credit ratings; they're not people with large savings. So I took my savings and my credibility and borrowed from the bank on my credit in order to have the money with which to build houses, more and more at one time, and provided the craftspeople with good jobs.

Developing Land

I discovered I could make a profit building houses. But if I could buy land and develop that land into lots, then I could make another profit on land development. And if I could get others to build those houses for me for a commission or for a personal profit, then I could lend them the money to build and I could make still another profit on the financing. So rather than one profit from building a home, I could make a profit from building, developing, financing, and selling–earn four profits in place of one.

I owned five acres so I bought fifteen more that my mother had inherited from the Kreider Estate. The price was one brand-new 1950 Ford sedan.

It was a four-door car that Mother picked out, and she was satisfied with this way to pay her for the land. I don't know why I've always remembered the colors: Seasprite Green and Snowshoe White, two-toned, green with a cream top. It probably cost in the neighborhood of five to eight thousand dollars, so I bought those fifteen acres for the price of her car.

Nowadays, an acre lot is too little to pasture a cow and too big to mow, so it would not be popular; most people want small lots. But back then, people liked what was called a sub-urban: a house with about a one-acre lot. So I built twenty hous-es on twenty acres, creating my first subdivision.

At that time it was outside the city limits. City Utilities called it Manley Drive because I was the one that developed it and I was the one that was living there, as far as ordering utili-ties and electricity and gas. There wasn't city water available yet, so I had to drill what we call a community well, and each of those twenty houses had a share in that well. It couldn't be done today. But it was a large system and that served for many years.

Manley Drive continues on in several locations south of there, like many older streets that have breaks, a cul-de-sac or a residential subdivision that was later developed.

After 1950, my wife, Jayne, was the one who maintained our at-home office, our only office until about twenty years ago when I had a mobile home that we moved to different loca-tions in the subdivision and had our business conducted from there, during normal business hours, but still from our home after hours. I moved into this office when this bank building was constructed, only about five years ago, because our busi-ness had become larger.

Jayne has always been great at taking care of business, such as answering the home phone and making appointments for people to come over after their work hours to receive an esti-mate on their home or to have plans drawn up.

I became so experienced that I could estimate at less than 1% of what a house was going to cost. Even with some vari-ables–an increase in the cost of lumber or windows or doors–I could add the price increase and still have the same rule to go by. That enabled me to have a profitable business because I knew what the product cost.

Making a profit enabled us to comfortably rear our daugh-ters and enjoy family life. We had excellent medical and dental care and excellent help with our children. We went to plays and PTA meetings. We would take the girls places and go watch them cheerlead and play in the band. What a blessing it was to have the children to share our life!

In fact, the oldest and youngest of our three daughters–who now are 50, 48, and 46, approximately–share the building and development business with us, not because we directed them, but because they chose to. The middle daughter is a school counselor.

I've built over 2000 homes since beginning in the building business over fifty years ago. I've built for three generations of people! I developed eighteen different subdivisions.

And once again my war experiences affected decisions I made later.

When I was in England preparing for the D-Day invasion of France, I was able to tour areas of historical significance, including London. There I could see, for example, the River Thames, Big Ben, the palaces, the Marble Arch, Kensington Palace.

I discovered I loved English architecture, and when I saw that some of their very ornate buildings had been destroyed with the bombs before D-Day, it brought tears. They were centuries old!

So I gave English names to many of my subdivisions, names that really had meaning for me because of my admiration and respect for English history that I acquired during the war.

I named Marlboro Manor and Marlboro Arms after the Marlboro Arch and the Duke of Marlborough. We began with Marlboro Manor 1st Addition; now we're on the 14th Addition, though I retired from that part of our business after the 12th Addition. Marlboro Arms is an apartment that I built across from Drury University on Benton.

Kensington, a time-honored, traditional name much like period furniture, became a subdivision. To have names as stable as Marlboro and Kensington–the idea was a hit! People knew about that; it was English tradition, English culture.

I have deep admiration not only for the architecture which we saw but also for the British people because of the sacrifices they went through in order to have the millions of soldiers there from other nations, as well as taking the bombings from the Germans each night! All of these things, individually and collectively, made me think: Gee, they have to be wonderful people to put up with this–sturdy, hardy stock like those that built America.

I admired the many people who lived in flats, what we call apartments. But because my farm background had provided me with so much yard and livestock and acreage, I knew I couldn't be cooped up like that.

My own home today is English Tudor and has the lookout window on the third floor with a light that stays on day and night. Near the coast areas, many of the homes were two-story, and in the very peak of the home they would have a lookout window. Maybe a spiral stairway went up there, if it was not two-story. They called it the Attic Window, to see the ships out on the English Channel. And the ships near the coast of England could see the lights on the shore and could head toward them.

"My family has given up trying to keep me from putting up our
Christmas lights to decorate our home."

Early on I designed most all my homes and I didn't copyright the designs.   In Jarrett Junior High School I had mechanical drawing with Chester Erickson. Mr. Erickson quit teaching at Jarrett and went to teach at Springfield High School, so I took every course he taught at the senior high. When I came back from the military service, he was teaching part-time at Drury College and there I took additional architectural drawing and courses like Descriptive Geometry from him. So nearly all the plans I drew myself, I learned from him.

Also at Jarrett I had woodworking with A. R. Cade, learning from him how to saw, to plane, to measure with fine instruments and to build cabinets. Because of Mr. Cade, I continued to have a desire for and interest in woodworking.

We formerly had to make concrete with a mixer by hand, but as we grew, we used a ready-mix concrete company, the Concrete Company of Springfield now called Conco. They started with three GI trucks, three army surplus trucks, because only the military service got any new trucks produced.

These trucks with dual wheels on the back held up to three yards of concrete in this large container. They mixed it up at the factory, drove to our location, turning and mixing the entire time. When we were ready, they would turn it in reverse and that would let the concrete come out a large chute into our foundations. We built our foundations in those days out of the lumber with which we were going to frame the house.

All along some of my subdivision, in part of my land development, we had donated land for the Greenway Trails.

As a matter of fact, we helped start that process whereby if there was land in the flood plain on which we could not build, then we would donate that land to the city for a Greenway Park, a Trail, along the creeks which at times might be flooded during the heavy rains. The city maintains the trails as part of our park system. I was not obligated or liable for accidents that might occur, because it was deeded to the city.

All my life since I've been in the business, around sixty years, I've helped with building codes and with land development codes, both in the county and the city. There was a time that, if a house was built in a flood zone, some sucker might come along and buy it, not realizing what might happen. And cities would have to buy the people out, in some of the flood zones. From Day One I always wanted to protect the people, so I would donate the land. I would even donate the land to build schools, so that they too could have part of the Greenway Trails to use for their biology or botany classes along the stream, and to check the water as far as the purity of it.

The average homebuyer wants to trust that his builder has done what is right and safe! So, again, in development we have learned to give the people what the people want in their homes, in the shapes and sizes and colors, and all the amenities of water and gas and sewers and sidewalks and fireplugs and streetlights. Even though the developer has to pay for all this, at the time he is developing, he will recover his costs as he sells the lots, the completed lots with all those amenities and with the finished house.

Our land development codes necessitate that we must have accessibility to sewers or we don't build! Certainly I wouldn't touch a piece of ground as far as building or developing unless we had access to sewers, and I wouldn't do it unless we had access to water.

This part of Missouri probably has more caves and sink holes than about any other area of the state, and since caves and sink holes affect our underground water supply, we shouldn't fill a sink hole with debris or put septic tanks in a heavy subdivision. We put sewer lines in so we can protect the water supply.

Now there have been times, in early development years, when the city water mains or city sewer lines were too far away and we had to have septic tanks on larger tracts of land; developers still could today on five or more acres. But a septic

"1950 Chevrolet, new for our honeymoon."

"Our first home, 1200 Stanford,
Springfield, Missouri, in 1950."

"Our first good truck, dark
blue Chevrolet, and our
first daughter, Janell,
around 1953."

"Our new Chevrolet truck bought for
$700 cash from Charles Terrell in
Ozark, Missouri, around 1956."

"I received my Master's
Degree in Business
Administration from Drury
College in 1969."

"My Chevrolet truck and me,
summer 1985."

tank must be treated with respect or it will not operate properly for very long.

We don't develop five-acre tracts anymore; we develop subdivisions where we have all the amenities. The average person who buys a home doesn't know how to protect a well in case of freezing in wintertime; doesn't know that with a septic tank, things can't be put down the drains as in a typical home that's on sewer with a garbage disposal.

We've learned that people want less work on a home, more serviceable products, so long ago we converted to all brick homes and vinyl siding, and aluminum soffits and overhang and fascia.

My Typical Day in 2005

I used to get up at 5:30 a.m. Now I wake up at 5:30, still as a matter of habit. I listen to the news and the weather. If it's raining I know what to do and how to plan my day. That used to be even more important because I would have workers and if it was raining, I wouldn't have them working the yard or putting on a roof; I'd have to schedule them to work inside a home, putting on the sheet rock or trim, for example.

"Here's a sign that appears in front of property for sale or lease."

I get up around seven and eat breakfast. A typical breakfast would be a bowl of cereal–usually with fruit cut up in it, bananas or strawberries–two pieces of toast, and a cup of coffee or a glass of milk. I probably like Raisin Bran or Frosted Flakes best. Sometimes I might have Mini-Wheats. In the wintertime, it might be oatmeal, because it's kind of a warming-type cereal.

Because I retired from building and now just manage a number of my properties, a typical day begins by checking on the properties I have vacant, and opening up the ones I have for sale or lease. I leave home about 7:15 or 7:30 to make sure the signs are out so they're ready for people to view.

I look for what might need to be done. We hire various people who will mow the yards, trim the shrubs, paint, repair or replace plumbing, and clean. We lose income when they're not occupied, and of course we want the income.

Then I come here to the office and go through the phone calls. Most of the time, now, I have the office phone transferred to my cell phone and I can say I have my office open with extended hours! I usually take the cell phone and that's been quite a blessing for me. I still believe in serving the customer, whatever his needs are.

A typical phone call might refer to an ad in the paper or to a yard sign that shows my firm name and phone number. A caller will ask: "What do you have to rent at this time?" I answer, "What would you like to have? I have several." I listen to the caller's needs and explain what I have. Other phone calls are questions regarding City Council business, other appointments regarding City Hall, and ribbon cuttings.

My daughter Jennifer works flex-time for me because I don't have all that much business where I need a full-time secretary. She takes her boys to school, and then she comes here and manages everything at the office. She usually gets here before I do.

She has everything computerized so we know whether or not a property is vacant, the amount of rent or income it brings, the monthly payments, taxes, insurance. This computerizing makes it relatively simple. Each day I print out a sheet she creates, so I keep current on what's for sale or for rent. At this particular time I probably have five empty, but out of 150 that's not bad!

Quite frankly, I have not learned much on computers because she does that for me. I do the other things, that I *do* do well, and she does the computer that *she* does well. We help each other, in that respect. It's a beautiful arrangement for both of us.

Today we went through a weekend's worth of mail, and listened to people's voice mail complaining about their air conditioner, or this, that, and the other. We always follow up on the phone messages as quickly as possible, if we can solve the problem. One woman said she found a snake in the yard and could we please come and do something about it, but that was on the answering machine from Saturday!

Jennifer and her husband, Skip, have their own business, also building and developing. If somebody wants something built, I refer it to them. Also, I'm working on a subdivision I've started down in Republic. There are about twenty-eight lots, so Skip and Jennifer are building me twenty-eight houses there. It wasn't family land; I just bought it. They have four houses going right now and keep at least four going all the time.

I don't and haven't become a slave to my business; it's not that demanding. If our twin grandsons have a ball game at Hillcrest, we'll be there. Jayne and I always have something to do, and we want to stay busy.

Home Builders Association

In 1954 we organized the Home Builders Association of Springfield. I was one of the charter members, so they recognized me with 50 years of service, in 2004.

"Janell and I were selected to emcee the November 2, 1999 Salute to Construction Awards Banquet. Springfield Magazine put us on their cover."

Greene County Commission

At first I couldn't serve the city because I was outside the city limits. I worked on the Greene County Building Commission then. I fought for years to help the county get building codes, zoning and planning, because I knew this was the way to go. But I was always interested in the city. Then they took me inside by annexation.

Springfield City Council

After they took me inside the city, then I had to go city route rather than county route. But it works really well, because the city and the county have to cooperate in many many ways.

We've seen a combination of city-county health departments; we've seen city-county libraries; we've seen city-county tax collection. I suspect the next thing we might see in the near future will be a combination of city and county building and planning and development services so we can have the same type of zoning. In the more distant future, I can see the city and county combined with one government.

Our county government, in my opinion, is set up as in the olden days when a person came to the county seat to pay his taxes or to record legal documents, and it needed to be within one day's ride by horse or buggy or wagon. We had commissioners to represent each portion of the county, with a presiding commissioner. Of course, that's very archaic anymore, too; we don't need that.

One county manager would be far better, but superior to that would be one city-county manager because then we'd have professional management, rather than people who are unskilled but who may be popular as far as the ballot box is concerned.

I worked with county government for years as a volunteer. There is also no pay for being on City Council. But I choose to do it in order to help the community. We hate to be governed by fools. The community has been very good to me; this is a great place; if I have an education, then I should be making these decisions, along with others who have knowledge of the past and visions of the future. I want Springfield to be better today than what it was yesterday. That's why I'm on City Council.

I attend a number of the council sub-committee meetings. Usually on Tuesday noon the City Council has a sandwich lunch at City Hall to go over the plans and policies and to have some of the departments present a program–whether it's the airport or the police or the fire or the planning and zoning–so we can keep up-to-date on happenings around. We have Agenda Sessions to go over the agenda for the following Monday–City Council meets every other Monday. We might go look at property that is on the agenda or drive around and see what changes we could make on zoning. Zoning cases are the ones that give the most problems. That's how it can take twenty to twenty-five hours a week, with committee meetings and viewing properties.

I've been on City Council six years. It's an elected position. I'm a native here and have quite a lot of visibility, so I've not had opposition when I've run, which I guess is unusual.

"I'm currently on the Springfield City Council"

I'll be 83 when I plan to run again. My health is good, I feel good, and I've been in business all my life, so I feel as though I can make prudent decisions.

I devote a lot of time to helping the community because this community has been good to me. I've made a great living here, and I've had a great family here. Just to give back some of my time to help make it a better community is a tremendous amount of joy for me.

Chamber of Commerce Ambassador

I go to a lot of ribbon cuttings and ground breakings for the Chamber of Commerce because I'm one of the Chamber of Commerce Ambassadors. You might say I'm an ambassador for the city as well, because I'm Mayor Pro-tem. I do this as a courtesy, as a means of saying, "Hey, we're glad you're here, we're glad you had this idea and put it into fruition." I do what I guess has become famous: with both arms raised high above my head and my hands wide open, I jump about a foot off the ground, straight up and down, to show enthusiasm and excitement for each new business. They love it!

"Here I am cutting the ribbon at the dedication of the new
McGregor Elementary School, January 2003."

Part 3

TEACHING BUSINESS, ECONOMICS, AND PATRIOTISM

Why did I teach? Because of the war, I'd seen the worst that could happen to human beings, but I'd also learned that by working with others, people can accomplish many, many things they could never do alone. I wanted to take the best that I'd learned and teach others to be positive rather than hate or criticize each day. I wanted to share my philosophy that all days are good; some are just better than others.

I especially wanted to teach young people: Hey, appreciate who you are, regardless of your economic or social circumstances. America wants you and needs you, and you are especially important to this community and to all your relatives and loved ones. You're unique, one of a kind!

Develop your talent because mediocrity really doesn't have much place in American society. Whether your talent is fixing an automobile or painting a beautiful picture or making a good grade on an exam or studying for class rather than watching TV, also enlarge your understanding of people so you can contribute to the joys and pleasures of all mankind.

You, the youth of America, are the cream of the crop with the most energy of any group, and should have the biggest dreams.

I'm the worst mechanic God ever created; I don't know anything about running a car; but how much I appreciate the auto mechanic who can keep my car running by analyzing and diagnosing any problem, and fixing it. Or the janitor who cleans this office room or a classroom: bless his heart. He's enabled me to work and think and do and promote and vision in cleanliness.

Everybody is important, even if you don't have much money. You can have dreams. Really, a student without a dream is poor indeed. I want you to have dreams, I want you to aim for the stars, I want you to be all you can be by developing those skills and taking those classes that will enable you to be better than what you are.

Drury Night School

About 1967 I started teaching a class in the evening division at Drury called "How to Buy or Build A Home," and being one who was actually in the business and had an "ongoing laboratory" every day, it really went well. I taught at Drury for three years in the night division.

One of the students was Dr. Vencil Bixler, head of the department of Finance and General Business at Southwest Missouri State University. He liked me.

(Southwest) Missouri State University

The person who was teaching Real Estate at SMS was retiring, so Vencil asked me if I would come over and teach. I said I'd be delighted to, because I really wanted to share my business knowledge as well as my patriotism and belief in America. Dr. Bixler was my department head the whole time I taught at SMS.

Teaching has given me the opportunity to share with young people the skills I learned first in college, then from actual building and buying and developing real estate. I had done well in my own business, so I truly believe I was a successful practitioner teaching those courses. I taught Real Estate and Finance at SMS for twenty years, the very thing I was doing in real life. I loved every day of it. I still love teaching.

Dr. Vencil Bixler

I went to SMS teaching full-time in 1969 and I retired from teaching in '89, only because I was 65 years old and that's when they want teachers to retire. I continued to carry on my building and real estate development business after retiring from teaching.

Teaching in college is not an 8-to-5 job. A college teacher has only two or three classes a day, but is expected to do research and publish and have a doctor's degree. Well, I didn't have my doctor's degree, but I certainly had years of on-site experience and was teaching the very thing that I was working on every day.

However, because the typical expectation for a college professor was to have a doctorate, I went to Harvard and took a course, thinking of maybe going there and getting my doctorate. I already had a Master's degree in Business Administration from Drury.

Most of the professors were talking with a foreign accent or a slur of the English that I didn't care for. I didn't fit in with the way Harvard catered to the princes and dignitaries of other nations, from where much of its donations came. I decided this one semester at Harvard was enough for me so I did not go anymore. It was a short course in the summertime, in the early '70s.

As part of the SMS college instruction, during Spring Break each year we would select the best group of students we could gather who were majoring in real estate or finance, and take them to New York City. There we would visit some of the biggest corporations: AT&T, at that time JC Penney, Metropolitan Insurance, the New York Stock Exchange, the Cotton Exchange, Citicorp. We'd eat in the most elegant Board Rooms we could ever see, with the fanciest of china. We'd tour the Statue of Liberty and always take in a great Broadway play; I've seen *Cats* about six or eight times.

We'd made pre-arrangements to visit those firms, so we divided up and studied them beforehand. One or two students would take one firm and present the research to the rest of the class, including the firm's history, products, services, and management background. So the whole class usually knew more about that firm than the firm's management knew! And with that type of knowledge we could ask intelligent questions when we visited and they always asked us back. I went to New York for about ten times, every other year, in the '60s and '70s.

At one point I was Director of Development. The public institutions had to raise private funds, because the legislature was not giving them the money they felt they needed. That job started out as half-time teaching, half-time fundraising, but it became full-time fundraising with a little teaching. It didn't set too well with me because I really loved to teach and it took me away from the students. I only did that for one year; I said, "I don't believe I care for this," so I went back to full-time teaching.

I would get very enthused and motivational with my teaching, because I cared for young people and wanted them to do well. I used the Eisenhower silver dollars to try and get across my point of teaching the students to get the odds for success in their favor. That meant to do research, to listen to what the people wanted, and to read what successful people have found to work for them. By combining these in their fields of endeavor, then they could be successful.

I'd say: "You can't be so selfish and greedy that you try to satisfy your own needs and that's it. Everyone is entitled to dignity and respect in America, and to have what he needs to raise a family and have a safe job. A number of people I served with during the war were from all walks of life. One of them was a convicted murderer who got out of the penitentiary by volunteering for the paratroops"–and I always make it very clear to my students, to add humor–"but that's not how I got there. He was important to me to accomplish the mission that we had. And helping others become successful is necessary to keep freedom in America."

A Typical One-on-One Mentoring Session

Case Real Estate in Marshfield is a name I've always remembered! James Hoover Case, here's one of my business cards, an Eisenhower silver dollar. When you look at it, remember that if you want to be successful in life, you've got to increase those odds that prevent failure.

Most businesses that start, fail. They don't plan to fail, they fail to plan. How nice it is if you increase those odds of success in whatever business you undertake. Sixty percent chance of being successful means 40 % chance of being a failure; 80% chance of being successful means 20% chance of being unsuccessful!

Nothing in life is for sure, but if you want to get the odds in your favor of being successful in whatever field you undertake, you must do it with education, with ongoing research, by following what successful people have found to work for them, and by listening to the needs of people.

What is a People Person? A People Person is one who can listen and understand and get along with people. Be a People Person! Then you can converse and help your customer. Our whole society is service: people helping people. By doing this, you're able to make a profit.

"James Hoover Case and me at Drury University in front of Manley Hall, formerly my Marlboro Arms Apartments."

Profit isn't a nasty word. It is essential for any business to survive. But the average person is a poor manager. He can't manage his time and he can't manage his money: you'll discover this to be true, if you haven't already. You will be successful by helping people who are uninformed. Anticipate their needs. Answer their questions honestly and completely. They buy real estate so infrequently that they aren't as familiar with it as you are. Have a genuine desire to help them find that real estate they're looking for. That's your role! You don't necessarily show them what you've got listed; you listen to what they want and help them get it.

I discovered early on that men look at the yard and garage; women look at the house and the kitchen inside. If you're meeting with a man and wife, talk to the wife. Women buy houses. Children are next; kids have schools they want. Men just want to please their family.

I've learned a lot from the automobile dealers, James. If I want a car, I can go to the automobile dealer and buy it. If I can't buy a new car, they have used ones; they have pickups; they have SUVs; they have convertibles; they have red ones, blue ones, green ones, white ones.

Besides that, most people don't have the money to buy a car. Very few cars are sold for cash. Well, they can finance it for you! They can sell insurance for it! See, in the car market, the automobile dealer can help you with it all—new, used, financing, insurance.

So I learned that in the real estate business, I can take a trade-in and I can have houses to rent. Renters are usually people who don't have enough money for a down payment or can't buy for some other reason. Most people, to qualify for a home loan, have to have a steady job and a steady income. They can't owe more than about 30% of their income for other debt. So if I have houses to rent, then I can help somebody. By expanding my market, I have more options to offer my customers: new houses, used houses, rent houses.

When I started in the building industry, because my grandfather on the farm taught me how to repair the stanchions and the barn doors, build an outhouse, a corral, to plumb and to measure and to saw, I had the basic needs for building. When I came home from the service in 1945, I was a young, unmarried man and I wanted to have my own home; I didn't want to live "at home" anymore. So I built a house and somebody offered me about $1500 more than the cost that I had in it. I sold it for just $5000. And I said, Well, I'll build another. So I built another. I've built over 2000 homes.

Then I learned as an Economics student at Drury about leveraging my time and leveraging my money. That meant using other people and other people's money to do what I wanted to do. If I could get other people to help me, I could build six or eight or ten houses a year. By myself I was building about four a year. To help build and finance these homes, I could go

"Here's an aerial view of some of my homes and subdivisions in Springfield"

to the bank and borrow money at 6%, work it and use it and make 15% to 20% on it, then pay the bank what I borrowed plus the 6% interest, and keep 14% for myself. That's the backbone of every business! Take the skill and desire that you have and put it to work.

James, as you grow and prosper, you will probably have to borrow funds. As long as you can borrow and make more than what the funds cost, then borrow. There were some years I didn't borrow any; I didn't build anything; I just did some remodeling. Why? Because rates were 21%! 21% interest for borrowing money! No one could borrow and pay that back! So those years I did remodeling and kept my crews busy. I wanted to hold together the craftsmen that I had, and they had families to support.

Later I learned an additional way to make a profit in the real estate business. I could develop land and convert it into lots, put in water, sewer, gas, streets, sidewalks, which as a developer I had to borrow funds to do. But I needed to start with a vision, a dream, choose a tract of land by first deciding how and where to put streets, thinking about the lay of the land and about how the water and sewers would flow and drain.

Springfield's sewage disposal system is southwest of town because that's downhill. Water runs downhill! So if I want to build houses and develop land and I want sewers within a reasonable distance, then I go south. Of course another consideration is that we have more caves and sinkholes in Missouri than in any other state, many of them right here.

If I have septic tanks–which is an individual sewage disposal system–it pollutes the water, and planning and zoning just won't let anyone have a subdivision on septic tanks anymore. That's out of the question. What's happened in the past has happened, but you can't put new ones in without sewers. So if I look for land, I want land I can put on sewer. And I don't want to pay for sewers running by the neighbor's property; I want it up to my land. I can't afford to pay for streets and sewers by the neighbor's land and then do my own too. He probably gets it for nothing! That doesn't work; I lose and he wins! I want sewer available to my tract of land.

A profit on building and a profit on developing the land gives me two profits, doesn't it. And if I develop the land and can get other craftsmen to help me build these houses, then the quicker I get that loan paid back, the less interest I pay, and the more profit I make.

These craftsmen don't have the money to build, so if I can borrow the money on my good credit and lend them money to build this house, then I can make the profit on financing too. That's three profits.

I've never built or had houses built that I want to build but ones I thought the customer wanted and would buy. Until that customer buys something, I won't even recover my costs, let alone make any profit. I learned that as a college student, too.

But a typical craftsman is not a sales person; he's not a People Person; he doesn't know the market for real estate; he doesn't know what financing is available or current interest rates;

he doesn't know who's in the market to buy or what the people want. He needs a sales person, like me.

So now I have four profits: development, construction, financing, and sales. Four profits in real estate but using other people and other people's money to do what I want to do: build and develop houses. Isn't that simple and elementary, James?

The car dealer makes more money on financing, trade-ins, and service than he does on the new cars. He gets an old car in, high mileage or whatever, he doesn't even want it on his lot; he'll sell it out to a used car dealer. I do the same thing with houses. If we get a junk house as a trade-in? Sure, I'll take it in trade, but I don't want to keep it. I'll trade it to somebody as junk. A good one that's clean and we can do some cosmetic decoration to make it good and make a profit? I'll keep it. Then a person who comes in and can't afford one of my new houses? I've got a used one I can sell. If he can't afford to buy it, I'll rent it to him.

By being able to take a trade-in, someone with an old house–let's say it's worth $50,000–can get a new house. He owes $25,000. He can pay $25,000 down from the equity in his old house, and buy this house and not even have any money at all! Equity, of course, is the difference between what he owes and what the property is worth.

He trades the equity in this old house for equity in the new house, gets him a loan on the new house–why, I've made a sale, haven't I? Accepting trade-in homes has let me scoop the market. I've traded for years, people who didn't even have money to buy these new homes.

That's what these car dealers taught me. Trade in your equity. Of course, these days there's 100% financing available, but the buyer better expect higher interest rates with that type of loan.

Land, labor, capital, risk: the old economic terms. Land is always entitled to rent; labor is entitled to a fair wage; money is always entitled to interest; the manager or entrepreneur is always entitled to something for his risk. The laws of economics are just as true now as ever.

The old hogs-corn ratio in economics, James, is what they taught me. Simple. If you bought hogs for $10 a hundred and corn was $8 a hundred, you couldn't afford to buy corn to feed the hogs. It wouldn't pay. But if hogs were $25 a hundred and corn were $2 a hundred, you could afford to buy the corn to feed the hogs.

It's just the same with money: if interest rates are high, you don't borrow. Interest rates are low, you borrow. If you can see your way to make a profit, you borrow…other people's money. It takes lots of money in real estate; real estate is finance-intensive. For borrowing money, you have to be honest, you have to be credit-worthy, you have to be responsible. So if I can have good credit, then I can borrow, and keep on borrowing, as long as I pay back and do what I'm supposed to do. Then I can help these other people grow and prosper, too.

If you're a young man starting out, you don't have much capital, so if I lend you the capital to build this house that I designed for you, good. You've got a job and sometimes I can share the profit with you, too, besides your weekly wage.

All these craftspeople want is a paycheck every Friday night. Some of them go out and gamble; some go out and drink, get drunk. Most are poor managers, uneducated, school dropouts, con artists, felons. You deal with lots of people with muscle in the real estate business, as far as construction, who are not college-trained with regard to the management of their money or their time.

So as a builder today, I hardly know how to build anymore. I have to be a manager. I have to manage people, to manage money, to persuade other people to come to work for me and do what I want to do, when I want it done, and for the price I'm willing to pay. That's what a modern-day builder does anymore.

When I started building, I built most of the houses by myself. Then I hired somebody to help me. Typically today it takes about seventy-five different people to build a house: the surveyor, the dozer operator, the foundation company, the gravel company, the framers, the roofers, the insulation people, the furnace and air conditioning experts, the painter, the wallpaper hanger, the flooring installers of linoleum, Formica, marble, tile–all these craftspeople on a typical home. So I have to be able to be a People Person, don't I?

That's another talent of Eisenhower's that I wanted to emulate. He was not a great military tactician. Matter of fact: they promoted him above a lot of others who were, because they believed he could unite the British, the Canadians, the Australians, the New Zealanders, the Polish, the French, the Belgians, the Dutch, and the Americans, into one fighting force, to beat Hitler. And he was very good at that! Eisenhower, the People Person, surrounded himself with great military tacticians who made decisions about the Navy or Air Force or Army and which would do what.

He was able to unite all these different cultures, backgrounds, and educational levels, with the most winning smile you ever saw. James, people love courtesy! People love a smile, so give it to them! And with the help of other people and other people's money, you can not only move mountains, you can build them!

Look at the bright side of things, James. I saw so much Hell, death, and destruction in war: it was horrible! To have a day with no bullets flying and sunshine, what a beautiful day that was. Avoid negative people like a plague! You won't get to first base by following them. People do not like a complainer, a griper, a bitch. They like a positive person. "Gee, if it rains, I'm going to have that pretty grass, and look what it's going to do to the fruit crop!" "It's going to make the hay we'll need for winter feed."

Search for positive people: those with a great attitude; those with an idea and a vision and have confidence in themselves. Knowledge and education help give that confidence, along with reading, listening to, and watching other people.

James, the world needs leaders-in-the-making, people just

like you, coming on. You have a dream, a vision: you want to make some money, to have a car, to have a home, perhaps to have a family, to travel. You can get it! It's all possible in America. It all depends on you. Your family doesn't limit how much you make or how much success you're going to achieve in life. Your professors don't. Your university doesn't. You're the only limitation you have. Reach for the stars! It's all there for those who want to stretch out and reach! You can become a millionaire just as fast, as quick as you want to be, if that's what your goal is. It's like a ladder: just get up there a step at a time.

You don't become a millionaire overnight. It's according to how much you want to work. Work is not really drudgery. Work is an opportunity to solve a problem! You know, I dug enough foxholes in the army–that's a hole in the ground so I could protect myself from all the shells and bullets–that if they were laid end to end, I would have had a canal from the English Channel to Paris!

Inherently people are lazy, so they look for an easier way to do something. When I first started building, we had to dig the foundation ourselves, dig down in there. I just hated to dig; it made my back sore; and it made me really tired. Well, there was this fellow who dreamed how to put a chainsaw on the back of an army surplus jeep and go along and dig a foundation trench. Then another fellow began using a tractor and a backhoe: gosh, that made it easy! You have to admire them for fulfilling their dreams. Anything in America that can make an easier, better job is open for you or anybody else.

I suspect in the future you'll see a lot of prefabricated parts. You see a lot now, particularly with trusses, with roofs, ceiling members of a house, wall sections. When I first started, Sears Roebuck sold houses in their catalog! Here was a picture of a house, and they had firms to make the wall sections of, say, four feet wide. You could buy as big a house as you wanted or as small as you wanted; here's the price for it. Sears didn't do well at it because of the high shipping charges. We do a lot of stick building today, but eventually more prefabricated parts will come.

We have what we call unskilled labor and we're not highly unionized in the residential field, so labor costs aren't that high. It's wide open for building.

It's wide open for sales. But without customers you have nothing. So probably a good way to start in the real estate business is as a sales person, because it's minimal outlay. If you've got about $300, you can take a real estate exam, get your license, be a licensed sales person who is permitted to sell real estate and collect a fee for doing it. But it doesn't tell you how to deal with people.

James, in college-you are going to go to Drury-you'll take some psychology courses, sociology courses, religion courses, even an art course. Why? They're going to blend in just like that for a better understanding of people and a better understanding of people's real estate needs.

It's elementary really. You've got to be able to help people with their problem, and in helping them with their problem, you solve your own-and that's a profit. Isn't that simple? But that's the way it is. If you want your profit right now, the customer is going to see that.

Too many real estate sales people are so intent on getting that commission that they forget to help the people, and they miss sale after sale after sale. And the average person who gets his license in real estate will fall out or drop out after the first two-to-four-year period. He can't sell; he doesn't have income; it's strictly a commission basis. He sells something; he gets part of the commission; he's beholden to a broker who gets some of it, too, for providing him a phone number and office space, advertising, things like that.

As you prosper and grow, you will learn the value of real estate, the demand for real estate, what is on the market for sale, what something sold for-all these things are knowledge and education and research. Once you know what property is worth, then you can be an expert in your town-but it doesn't make you one in Springfield if you work in Marshfield. Or if you work in

Branson, it doesn't make you an expert in Springfield.

The key is understanding. You have to listen to their needs. If somebody would come in here this morning and want to buy a house from me, I'd say "Sit down, let's talk. What do you want? How much money do you have? What do you want to pay? Where do you work? What's your family? How many kids you got? What schools are they in?" All these things, because the better I know, the better I can help him get the very house he wants in the very location he wants with the money he has to pay. If you're sick and go to the doctor, he wants to talk with you and say, "How do you feel today? Where do you hurt? How's your breathing?" He has to listen to you before he can help. All right: a real estate person, as a sales person, has to listen to people before he can help them.

"How much do you want to pay? How much savings do you have?" All these things. If some of it gets too personal, you don't want to say: "How much money do you have?" He might say, "Well, that's personal. I don't have to tell you that." Then you can say, "How much are you willing to put down on the house?" or "How much are you willing to pay for a monthly payment for a loan?" See, just wording things a little bit differently so you don't get too personal, too private, makes a difference.

And always with a positive attitude; always with a smile; always courtesy. People crave courtesy! Give it to them and you've got a customer!

There are all kinds of banks in town. You can take your money any place you want. But the one who gives you the most courtesy, the one that can call you by name, the one that has various services gets your business. You want a loan for a car? They can help you! You want a loan for a home? They can help you! Just need some money for thirty or sixty days? They can help you! You want to put some in there for savings? They can help you! They're geared to help the customers. Without customers, they'd have nothing.

What property is worth, listings, what's for sale, what sold, what did it bring–all this is public knowledge anymore and with computers it's right at your fingertips. That's why you need your basic computer skills, because you can get all the appraisals from the assessor's office.

If the assessor has a property appraised for $125,000, and the owner paid $100,000 for it, he's going to raise hell and appeal his property assessment by going before the appeal committee to try and get it lowered, to lower his taxes. However, if a $100,000 house is listed by the assessor's office for $90,000, the owner thinks, "Ho! I gave more than that, it's worth more than that," and says nothing. You'll discover, James, the assessor's value is usually under market because if it's over the market, property owners are going to raise Cain and say the assessor is the most rotten guy they've ever seen and there will be long lines stacked up at the assessor's office, trying to get the Board of Equalization to lower their taxes.

Life is so full of opportunity! So full. There are always people who want to sell real estate and there are always people who want to buy real estate, regardless of conditions. Things change: death; change of jobs; divorces; ill health; job opportunities. All these things are elements that may influence real estate for market, for sale.

For example, you, James, will discover at Drury in Economics that if the average wage for a typical work person in this town is, say, $7 an hour, then for a forty-hour week it would be $280. Typically, a person can afford one-fourth of his income for housing costs. A house always has utilities and taxes, so one-fifth of your income for house payment, one-fourth of your income for housing costs. So if you make $280 a week, that's about $1200 a month. How much house can you afford? You're going to have to rent a cheapie, aren't you. So you're not going to build $200,000 houses for people who can only afford $240 a month, are you. You learn people.

You learn what market you're building for. If I built all million dollar houses in this town, I'd go broke! What is the market here?

Well, typically, we have man and wife both working. Two incomes. Maybe they're both making $1000 a month, and maybe they can afford $500 a month payment. So I could probably build $80,000 to $100,000 homes and fill that market, couldn't I.

You structure your building and the homes you have for sale to those who have the funds to buy. You don't build a whole bunch of million dollar houses on a "spec" basis, because the market just can't do it. For example, right now in Spring-field, Missouri, there are over 1500 apartments under construction. Currently we can absorb about 400 a year. With 1500 under construction, you know what's going to happen? The new ones, in their desperation to get some income, might rent on a month-to-month basis, rather than a year. They might give a free color TV to move in today. People prefer clean to dirty and new to old. The price being the same, the new one's going to rent but the old ones are going to hurt the market. Some of the new ones might be hurt, too, because they may not want to lower their standards to rent on a month-to-month basis. We've got too many under construction. We can't absorb that many that fast. This is research!

If mortgage interest rates are 20%, how many houses do you think you are going to sell? Nine out of ten homes have mortgage loans on them, so you're not going to sell any new homes, I can tell you that. Now if interest rates are 6%, you're going to sell some new homes, aren't you. So when interest rates are high, the rental market is there; when interest rates are low, the buying or for-sale market is there. Research! Know what's happening! Keep in tune with interest rates, housing prices, lumber prices.

For example, notice the lumber yard! Right now they have lumber stacked up in containers, double and triple stacked, as high as a fork lift can reach. Why? Because there's going to be a tariff on lumber from Canada and we get much of our lumber from Canada. So with a tariff on it, that makes it higher, so they've stocked and increased their inventory before the tariff goes into effect. And they've got lots of lumber that they're paying interest on, because they've had to borrow money to pay for it, but that's less cost because of low interest rates than paying the tariff. Makes sense, doesn't it.

All these things fit together, but you have to be a manager that can take land, labor, money, and your risk and put it together in a recipe for profit. If you took two eggs and a cup of milk and a cup of flour and a cup of sugar and a dash of vanilla and put it in a mixer, you'd have a beautiful cake. But let's take the same ingredients: how about a cup of vanilla, a cup of eggs, a pinch of flour? No one would want to eat a cake like that at all, because it's not tasteful. So it's up to you as a manager of any business–land, labor, capital, and your skills–to make that recipe for profitability.

If interest rates are high? I don't build; I don't borrow. Lumber is high? I might look for something else that's different, or build fewer "spec" houses. Keep up on what's happening in the market. Listen to people. Read the paper. Know interest rates.

The average person doesn't know, really, what price a house ought to be; he doesn't know how much he ought to pay for housing; he doesn't know the price of lumber. You're the expert in your field. That's why they look for you to help them with their housing problems. The average person doesn't know what houses are for sale or the prices of them or how many bedrooms or bathrooms a house has. Incidentally, with this same computer, you can get from the assessor's office not only the appraisal of a house; you can get a complete floor plan, that tells you how many bathrooms; how many bedrooms; how many fireplaces; whether it has a basement or not. All that information right there free of charge, for you, when you know how to use that computer. So if somebody asks, "Well, how many bedrooms does it have?" you can answer, "Well, it has three bedrooms and they're nice-sized."

That's why, as a sales person–you're going to sell first, that's the starting point–you prosper and grow, then you get your broker's license and you can operate on your own and not have to split that commission with anybody else. And then as you grow, maybe you can get other people to work for you.

I had a fellow just this year say, "You know, I'm just working for all my sales people. I'm not making a bit of money. I'm furnishing their office space, they're lazy, they're not producing anything, and I have to dig money out of my pocket every month just to pay for everything we have at the office. What should I do?" And I said, "Close the office. Get rid of them and close the office."

All of us have to work to make a living. Work is so satisfying if you enjoy doing what you're doing. People rarely succeed doing things they don't enjoy. I enjoy real estate. Every house is different; every transaction is different; every financing is different. It's not monotonous at all. I can see it grow. In three months' time I can see a vacant lot become a finished house. It's exciting!

Selling real estate helps you accumulate some savings, some capital. Whatever you make, save some of it. By getting in the habit of thrift and savings, then you can accumulate some savings that lets you take advantage of an opportunity to buy a piece of real estate. If you see a real estate that's been run down and needs some cosmetic controls, weeds growing up, or maybe the guttering is falling down, you look at it and say, "Gosh, with a little bit of labor here, I can fix it up and decorate it up, maybe with a pair of shutters or some sod or some shrubbery or flowers, maybe new carpet or paint, I can take this and make a profit."

I make a profit on every house! Every house I take in trade, I make two profits: on the new one and on the old one. I can look at the trade-in and tell what it needs to be desirable. Everybody can't afford a $200,000 house! Maybe a $100,000; maybe $75,000. I've got something for everybody, remember? I've got a broad market here. "You want a $75,000 house? I can do it!" I have this trade-in house I just fixed up. That's all they can afford? Sure. Help them with it. Helping people with their problems. Isn't it simple to succeed in life?

You're signed up to take a real estate sales class next month with Vernon Kohl? He took every class in real estate that I taught at SMS. His wife, also. He retired from the Air Force, married a widow, and they've lived happily ever since. He lives in a subdivision that I built.

You're on the right track beginning as a sales person. Watch for sales, price of lumber, interest rates, and where to get loans. Develop the habit of thrift, and that's the starting place so you can buy a house that's in foreclosure, for example. Always have the title company research the title. Sometimes they have two or three mortgages on a property, totaling more than the property is worth.

I didn't start there because there hadn't been any houses built all during the war. When I got out of the service, materials were hard to get, because all had gone to the war effort, to build army camps, whatever.

The industry has changed! It used to take a carpenter all day to hang seven doors in a house. Then there was an easier way. They decided, on a bench in a factory, they could hang that door, have a split jam, put on the trim and finish it, and deliver the door unit. In the factory they could build a hundred door units in one day. So now the carpenter could hang twenty-five doors in one day, not just seven. See what progress can do? That's life. Take advantage of opportunities.

Emerson once said: "This time, like all times, is a very good one, if we but know what to do with it." Education and research and more education will teach you what to do.

The average person who doesn't go to college doesn't learn about the whole economic system–land, labor, capital, management–doesn't know how to be a people person, hasn't had the knowledge and training to get along with others. In the military service, we'd see a sergeant who would force us, yell at us, get right up in our faces, ridicule us, make us feel stupid.

You don't do that with people any more! They don't have to work for people who don't treat them with respect, kindness. Of course, if they don't produce, obviously you have to get rid of them and get somebody who will produce.

You're not obligated to find a job for people; you're obligated to make a profit for your firm. If you don't, the money's gone; the firm is gone. What happens? You have to go to work for somebody!

I was your age, James, nineteen in the military service. By the time I was twenty I'd seen a lot of death and destruction. But we have a free America. We're living in the greatest nation on earth. We are living with more dignity and respect than any people on earth. Our government wants us to have clean water to drink, clean air to breathe, a safe job, a decent home, a good education, equal opportunity. No other government on earth is like America's. Americans really are the most envied people on earth because of all we're offered.

We have the largest middle class of people of any nation in the world. Why? Because our government wants us to have a good education. Here you're required to go to school, aren't you. Most countries don't even have a school for young people. We're rich in natural resources. We have about five percent of the world's population and about fifty percent of the wealth. In America. Why? Because of our ability to get an education, to dream, to send rockets to the moon. We'll find a cure for cancer. We'll find a cure for the common cold. We'll find a cure for many things like this because of young people like you!

Motivational Speaker

A person I've wanted to emulate is Jim Craig who was the head of the Better Business Bureau here for many many years. Jim was quite a sought-after speaker because he is very enthusiastic, very positive, very likable. He shared patriotism as I wanted to share it. He's older than I, lives here in town and is also a native. He's a fine man.

As a young boy I was bashful. It made me tremble if I had to speak before a group! But from people like Jim Craig and Eisenhower I learned to speak without trembling. Now I love to speak to groups; it doesn't make me nervous; it makes me excited because I can share those things that I really want to get across.

In every speech that I make, patriotism is going to creep in because I'm so happy and proud to be American. We're free to speak out for certain causes without the risk of being put in jail or being shot; to select a vocation; to get an education; to move from place to place, from state to state, without a passport, without an inspection station; to manufacture; to enter into a business; to live where we want; to develop the friendships we want. Because America's about a search for a better way, we benefit from our dreams, ideas and inventions, and have the highest productive system in the world.

I encourage people to be successful by enjoying what they do and doing what they enjoy. They can get better and better if they pay attention to the needs of people and to how successful people perform.

In many nations this is not true! Here, it's so wonderful. Once we have all these freedoms, we never want to give them up. Once we've enjoyed them, we'll fight for them, even the freedom to walk up and down the street peacefully, to greet the neighbors without the fear of retribution, without the fear of being taken by guards to concentration camp or a police station.

Life has been good to me because of the ethics my grandparents taught me: whatever you make, save some of it; if you want to get the odds in your favor, you research, educate, inquire, look, listen to other people. That enabled me to make the right investments the vast majority of the time so I could be able to prosper and grow.

Real estate has been far better for me than any of the stocks, because that's my study, that's my research, that's my training. For example, one of my friends in the stock brokerage business said, "Have I got a real hot deal here! For $17,000 you

"Jim Craig and Eisenhower, two of the people I've tried to emulate."

can get you these shares, and it's going to go!" Well, I put $17,000 in those shares and today those shares are worth about $7,000 and I've received nothing from them. Now that's what stock can do. I never have that rate of return on real estate, I can assure you! I have very little stock; just some with local banks, that's it.

People! The greatest single thing that you could develop at a university or in any class or in life is the ability to understand and get along with people. Eisenhower accomplished our mission because of his ability to organize and cultivate the various cultures in combination with his wisdom to surround himself with experts.

I try to avoid being around people who complain and bitch and gripe because that's not me. I want them to look for the good things and be thankful for what they do have! If they have a decent home, be thankful for that; a decent car, be thankful for that; a family, wonderful! Capitalize on the skills that we do have and look towards the brighter side of life.

Every day is a good day for me; some days are just better than others; there are no bad days.

Part 4

ANCESTORS, CHILDHOOD, UPBRINGING, AND EARLY EDUCATION

Why me? It's such a mystery in life, how some of us survive and how some don't. I don't know the answer. Sometimes, it's being in the right place at the right time…or the wrong place at the wrong time.

Someone who was reared in the city was probably not as good a soldier as one brought up on a farm. What I learned on a farm about sneaking up on animals helped me have a basic, perhaps better, knowledge for going through towns, house-to-house fighting, protecting myself around a ditch or tree or the edge of a building.

Sometimes it made the difference between life and death for me. It gave me a competitive edge, and I am thankful.

Ancestors

My great-grandfather on my mother's side, Kreider, came to this part of the country in the last of the 18th century from Reading, Pennsylvania, bought a section of land, and had five sons. His five sons were John, Tom, William, Jacob, and George.

When each son would get married, he was deeded forty acres of land. They would have a Building Bee and build a two-room house. So those five sons each had forty acres and a two-room house given by their parents. Each son's wife would bring in the Hope Chest with the linens, the dishes and the pots and pans, and the recipes, to establish this home.

Great Grandfather would lend each son a team of mules so the son could go and plow and till the field, the soil, on his forty acres. Because a team of mules was in great demand and cost about $600–lots of money for those days–he couldn't afford to give a team of mules to each son.

As those sons matured and had their families, the land eventually changed owners, some even before the son's death. Several sold out and went to the factories; others went to the Gold Rush and lost everything.

The son named John was my grandfather, John Phillip Kreider, and he married my grandmother, a local person, named Mary Victoria Elizabeth Harrington. They had two children, my uncle Rex and my mother, Helen Irene.

Except for military service and a short period when I first got married until I could get a house built there, I've lived on Grandpa Kreider's land all my life. When my grandparents passed away, Mother and Uncle Rex inherited, so I bought land from my mother first and built the home there, for my wife and me. Then, because he was quite a horseman and quite a bird dog fancier, Uncle Rex moved away to another farm, a place where he could have this on his own. So I bought land that he had inherited.

I was able eventually to purchase all the land that my grandfather first owned. I bought it at one time or another and built on all of it. I've built over a thousand homes out there on that land!

Childhood

I had an identical twin brother, Roland, and two sisters, Dorothy Frances and Mary Louise. Dorothy was born December 21, 1921, and Mary Louise was born in January, 1919. Roland and I were born October 15, 1923.

On the 4th of July, we could always count on a large container, about five gallons, of either chocolate, strawberry, or vanilla ice cream, for a great gathering of some of the neighbors and all the families at my grandparents' farm. And a case of soda pop of mixed flavors. At that time Model Markets were the forerunners of the supermarket, maybe a dozen locations in town, and they had pop that was two bottles for a nickel. What a delight that was to be able to really "step out" and have ice cream and soda pop at the same time!

One 4th of July the family had gathered at my grandparents' farm to eat ice cream and drink pop and shoot fireworks. Their roads were gravel in those days, and the person who delivered the evening paper from Springfield was delivering it on his motorcycle. I was about six years old, and liked to ride a horse to go and get the cattle on the farm. My older sister Mary Louise was on the back of the horse with me. Suddenly the motorcycle turned over after coming around the corner and sliding in the gravel, and that frightened the horse, the horse jumped, and my sister went over backwards. The horse's hooves hit her and fractured her skull, and she died in the hospital a couple hours later. Mary Louise was about eleven years old then.

That was my first experience with death. There was nothing we could do about it.

My parents got divorced after Mary Louise died from the fall from the horse, but I don't think her death was the reason. I'm not sure why they divorced. I wasn't around my parents enough to know if they expressed differences of opinion or argued or verbally abused each other.

I was around seven years old, when my parents divorced, so I lived with my mother's parents, John and Mary Kreider, at the edge of town in Springfield, Missouri, because they needed the help on their large dairy farm, about 250 acres of land. My twin brother worked there some, particularly during the summer and fall season. He and my sister Dorothy lived in town with my mother. My grandfather said, "One boy is a boy, two boys is half a boy, and three boys are no boys at all." He believed that when two boys get together, they want to play and maybe do a little work, and you get three, they all want to play and there's no work done. My brother and I had a tendency to play, I guess, and so my grandfather thought one would be better than two, and I enjoyed the outdoors more than Roland.

Ralph and Roland Manley,
born Oct. 15, 1923

Ralph, Dorothy, and Roland Manley, May 1932

Upbringing

My grandfather worked for the Frisco Railroad in Springfield; it was very large at that time. During the Depression years, it was a steady job for many people. People who worked at the railroad and the post office and city utilities were really stable, because the Depression had quite an impact on the economy here. He was not an engineer; he was not a conductor; he worked in the Frisco repair shops.

He was laid off during the Depression years, and devoted all his time to the farm. He had lots of tools. He taught me how to saw and how to plane and how to plumb and how to square, using lumber and the hand saw. So I learned the basic rudiments of carpenter work and building from him on the farm. We built corrals for the cattle or chicken roosts for the chickens or an outhouse. In addition, I learned to harness the team, and how to plow and disk the fields.

I can recall one of the first big bruises I had was looking between the bars of a hand-plow with a team of mules, and it hit a rock that made the plow hit me by the side of the head, since I was so small, and knocked a big bruise on my cheek, and I remember teaching myself: "I want to avoid that in the future! I'll stand farther back from the plow handles."

I enjoyed learning it all. It was outside work. I could see nature at its best as far as cattle and the calves. This was exciting for me. Town was not really to my liking. My brother liked it better; I think he was more for being around people, at that time, than I was.

Of course, I've since changed, you understand!

Early Education

I lived with my grandparents most of my childhood and high school years. We would get up early, four o'clock in the morning, and go get the cows from the pasture and put them in the barn, put the feed out for them, then milk by hand–before the days of milking machines. Then we'd go to the house, eat a big, hearty breakfast, I'd change clothes quickly, jump on the bicycle, and ride to school.

I went to McGregor Elementary School in Springfield to be with my brother. We were always together that way. We were together every day except maybe Saturdays and evenings. The address I used was my mother's, which was in town in the McGregor School District.

There was a county school closer to the farm: Sherwood Elementary School. It's still there, but it's part of the city school system now; it was absorbed into Reorganized School District of R-12. My grandsons have gone there, but of course it's a newer building. It was built way back when, but has gone from a one-room school to a rock school with several rooms. At that time it was fine, but today it's too obsolete. It's been added on to a number of times, with a library and a cafeteria and things of that nature.

I was six years at McGregor School. I would ride a bicycle from the farm, at the southwest edge of Springfield just west of where Horton Smith Golf Course is today, to McGregor, at the corner of Madison and Fort Streets.

And then immediately after school, I'd get on the bicycle, ride back to the farm, change clothes and start milking the cows. After the milking I'd take the cows to the pasture and help process the milk from the day. After supper I'd study whatever lessons I had, and then go to bed. What a day that was! A full day!

There was one time–again, Roland and I were identical twins–I did something wrong, I don't know what it was, and I was supposed to stay in after school. Well, I needed to get home on my bicycle to help with the milking of the cows, so my brother stayed in for me and the teacher never did know the difference! He did that for me! I probably was talking in class or something; it wasn't anything serious.

At McGregor School during the fall, I remember recess, shooting marbles. I couldn't do that on the farm. There was nobody to play with there, for one thing, but also no area to shoot marbles. On the school grounds it was almost bare; they had sand. I recall in the spring, we always would circle the tall Maypole holding large strings of different colors that were attached to it at the top. We'd weave the Maypole, in and out, girls and boys both. If there were twenty-five in the class, there'd probably be twenty-five strings. At McGregor there was always something to look forward to, even taking a trip, maybe to the zoo.

My grandparents and I were very much homebodies. Because I had to be at the farm to help with the chores, I didn't have those extra curricular activities after school that others might have had. I had to go home to work. Times were hard in those days; there wasn't much money around. Oftentimes, particularly in the spring of the year, we would go to school bare-footed and in our overalls.

I would have started to McGregor in 1928 or 1929. There were six grades there. No kindergarten; they didn't have it in those days. Mrs. Woods was the principal, Mrs. Dingledine was the 3rd grade teacher, Mrs. Jones was the 5th grade teacher,

Mrs. Elliff was another teacher there, Mr. Hanson was the jani-tor. All of them were wonderful people.

Probably my favorite subject in elementary school was Geography. I'd never been out of the city, much less the state! We hardly traveled in those days; we didn't have the money or cars that we have today. Geography taught me about Egypt and Mesopotamia, and the Tigris and Euphrates Rivers–ones that are in the news today because of the areas where we have been and still are fighting.

Then I went three years to Jarrett Junior High School, 7th, 8th, 9th grades, here in Springfield. I was intrigued with wood-working and mechanical drawing. The teachers were very good. Mr. Cade was the woodworking teacher: big fellow with a rough voice but a fine man. Mr. Erickson taught mechanical drawing, and from there went on and was to be my mechani-cal drawing teacher at Senior High and after the war at Drury. Those two teachers had quite a bearing on what I chose for life, what I enjoyed the most, and that was building and devel-oping and drawing plans.

During that time, I stayed with my grandparents, and I was the only other one in the house. It was a nice home, a big two-story home, and Grandma was a good housekeeper and a good cook. Of course there was no air conditioning, and when it got hot in the summertime, we might sleep on a pallet–a pillow and blanket–under a shade tree out in the yard, because it was cooler that way.

Those weren't the good old days; the good old days are today! But at least we survived without air conditioning; we survived without all the medicines we have today.

They had all those things that were necessary to have a bal-anced diet: Irish potatoes and sweet potatoes; apples, grapes, pears, plums. We didn't have celery or broccoli or cauliflower, but we did have radishes, onions, lettuce, beets, and carrots. Grandma would do a lot of home canning of the vegetables, especially green beans or corn, and there were times I helped.

But they might have much more of the vegetables than what we could consume or can, so they would dig a hole about a foot deep and about seven feet in diameter, put layers of straw in the bottom, pile carrots, turnips, potatoes, maybe even a few cantaloupes or watermelons on one edge, cover it over with straw, and put dirt over all of it. Then when the temperature was below freezing, they didn't freeze. We always had "fresh" vegetables in the winter!

Grandma did not have what is called a storm cellar. Her brother, my great-uncle, Roy Harrington, had a storm cellar that stuck about three feet above the ground, was made out of masonry or rocks and mortar, and in that he would keep his apples and sweet potatoes and Irish potatoes, and they would keep all winter. If they would go to sprouting in there, we'd have to go and take all the sprouts off the potatoes; if we didn't, the potatoes would be ruined because they would shrivel up.

I can say even during the war years she always had plenty of food. The only shortage she had that I recall was one of sugar or syrup. The Black Market was taking place in those days, and I think one time she traded a pig for a hundred-pound bag of sugar, Black Market Sugar somebody had gotten whatever way. Rationing was on in the early 40s.

This way of life taught me: if I want something, prepare for it. Because that's what we did. I wonder, even today, what my children might do, if they were put in the wilderness and told, "Now this is your home, eat what you can, where you can." I think they might starve to death!

My grandparents also taught one thing that has always stayed with me: whatever I earn, save some of it. Don't spend money foolishly–if I need something, fine; if I don't need it, then it's not a bargain whatever price it is.

My grandfather was a very thrifty man, and my grandparents during that day were wealthy–at least they were not on any government programs, they always had plenty to eat, they always had money to "do." The dairy brought in money, they had their own groceries and crops and things of that nature. It had a good influence on me!

Grandfather taught me not only thrift but responsibility. If I borrowed a tool, put it back. If I saw trouble when I was taking care of the cattle-they might be calving-to help the mama cow or get help from him or Uncle Rex.

Rex Kreider, Sr., was my father in as much time as I spent with him on the farm; I did not spend much time with my real father, ever.

Helen T. Buskett was Uncle Rex's wife. Aunt Helen would oftentimes prepare lunch for me, when I was a student going to either McGregor or Jarrett when my grandmother, for whatever reason, may not have. I preferred Helen T.'s lunch, because she had a nice little paper sack and it wasn't biscuits, it was sliced "light bread" and not lunch meat but jellies and sandwich spread. She might put a handful of raisins in there; she was one that kept raisins all the time. Oftentimes I'd put the lunch in my jacket pocket or between my shirt and my jacket as I would ride my bicycle.

Rex and Helen Kreider had five children and lived on the farm, too, but in a different house. Their five children were somewhat younger than I. He did the major work on the farm. Uncle Rex taught me how to milk a cow-and I think I was one of the best cow milkers around. I learned the responsibility of getting up early, getting the feed, making sure they had water, and turning them out to pasture.

Oftentimes they might have a hired man, a man who lived in what we called the bunk house, behind the large main home, who would do some of the farm chores as needed, particularly in the summertime when we had not only the dairy to take care of but also the plantings, and in the early fall when we had all the preparations of the meat for the winter.

One of these hired hands was Charley Myers. Coming through the Depression days, it was good for hired hands like

Charley to have a place to live and food to eat. I also learned from him to be able to do things in a different way. When he would go to town maybe on Saturday nights–and that's about when they had a chance to go, on Saturday night–he would put his clothes between the mattress and the box springs, to press them. Also, when my grandparents would kill geese, he would save the feathers and soon he'd have enough for a goose-feather pillow!

Charley Myers, long gone, was almost like family. He ate with us a lot; that's where his meals came from. He played a French harp, and I thought he was excellent. How he knew the tunes! He chewed tobacco, and sometimes he'd have to clear himself of tobacco before he could play his French harp.

He got married in some of the later years there, and he and his wife moved into a tent down on a hillside on part of the farm, near a creek and a spring. That way he would bring the cows up from pasture as he came to milk in the mornings and then in evenings take the cows down to pasture and go on home to the tent.

In the wintertime of one year, he stoked up the fire with a little stove he had in the tent and the sparks flew out on the top of the tent and burned little holes in it. It made a problem for him, so we had to get and melt wax and seal the tent so it didn't have all those little holes. And that even came to my mind as we were in England getting ready for D-Day, out at the lawn of the large country castle. We had little stoves there, about eighteen inches in diameter and just about that tall, but they used coke, and if we pokered that up, sparks would go outside of the little four-inch stove pipe, out through the top of the tent, and I knew right off that would not work because of Charley Myers's tent; we shouldn't stir up a little stove that would cause sparks to go out. So we never had holes in our tent!

I learned these things that helped me all through the war, and after!

Also I learned–as we would go in dark of morning, thick of

wintertime, to get the cows from the pasture–we could tell where the cows were by the sound of them walking or the sound of them clearing their throats. And we learned, as they might be silhouetted against the moonlight, a horse gets up on its front feet first and a cow gets up on its back feet first, so we could look and see which ones were the horses or the team of mules, different from the cows, by seeing how they were getting up. And by the sounds we could tell where they were. And as we would call them, they readily would come up to us. We knew to separate the horses from the cows.

It's one of the things I attribute my being able to carry through the war: our eyes and our ears were the things that would keep us alive. We needed to know every sound, plane, tank, gun, so distinctly that it was very clear whether it was the enemy or our own. I already had learned that on the farm, from those livestock!

And we would get the feed out, called silage, where they would gather stalks of corn with wagons. The neighbors would get together, lend a man a team and wagon to help the other neighbor fill silo. Each of them had a different wagon, none of them was rubber-tired in those days, and some of them were big high-wheeled wagons. And my grandfather taught me the reason that they had the big high wheels: as they'd go through the soft, muddy roads, it almost took that in order to keep the wagon from dragging bottom, particularly in the wintertime, with thawing and freezing.

But even though they had different farmers with different types of wagons–and different types of philosophies–they at least had one common thing and that was helping the neighbor.

As we would fill silo it would grind the corn and blow it up into pipes about eight inches in diameter and into the top of the large concrete silo. It was the way to store the grain, the silage, the cut corn, until we used it. And this one silo was enough to feed the cattle all winter at this dairy farm.

The fellow with the silage cutter was a custom farmer, he didn't farm himself, he just had the custom machinery to go to a number of farms as they filled silo or thrashed their wheat or oats. He had both the thrashing machine and the silo fillage machine.

Always, when we filled silo or when we thrashed the wheat, we would first go to town and, through the Labor Bureau, get a number of people to come out for just that day to cut the corn and process it. I recall in those days it wasn't really a lot to pay because some of them got seven or eight dollars a day for that, but it might have been a twelve-hour day!

Grandmother would have several women come in before lunchtime and they would help fix this huge meal for fifteen to twenty people, all neighbors, all working people, all men incidentally. The women at that time didn't work in the fields; the women would prepare the food.

I'd never seen so much fried chicken in all my life. As a younger boy I would have to eat in the kitchen and let the men sit at the table, and I would get the wings or the gizzards–I didn't get a breast or a drumstick or a thigh! A typical dinner might include, besides the fried chicken, breaded tomatoes, corn, green beans, and peaches or sweet potato pie for dessert. It was always stuff she had on the farm, but it was always a grand feast. It would remind anyone of a Thanksgiving feast today. This was one of the times that the dining room was filled and all the people were there, visiting and eating. How I enjoyed that!

One of these times I was taking the cows down to the pasture and I was throwing a rock across the road at a cow that was lingering on the road, and it just so happened that the rock hit one of these cars of one of these people who helped with the silo filling and all, and he didn't like it, so he told my grandfather about it. My grandfather took me by the suspenders of my overalls and he hung me on the back of a tall dining room chair! And I always remember that chair for that. I don't know how long it was, but it was to teach me not to throw rocks, even at the cattle! I had no intention whatsoever of hitting that car, I tried to tell my grandfather but he didn't listen. I threw the rock and I shouldn't have!

For thrashing, we always gathered up the bundles of wheat and oats together and put them in shocks to let them dry and cure. The binder would go along, and it would always take three mules or horses to pull that binder because it was a heavier load and had the large bull wheel in the middle of it. It was difficult! Sometimes we had to catch the weather just right so the wheat or oats would be dry enough, yet the ground would be dry enough so the bull wheel wouldn't sink into the mud. As the binder would come along and bind the wheat or oats in bundles, we'd come along and gather ten or twelve bundles into a shock. We'd bend two bundles by creasing them over our knees, to fit on top of these bundles as a cap, and leave the shocks to cure and dry for a month or two.

Then, in a few months, the fellow that had the custom farm tractor would come along with his thrashing machine and thrash the shocks. And of course thrashing was when we would gather together the farmers–helping each other once again–to load the shocks onto the wagon, bring the wagon up to the thrashing machine so the thrashing machine could thrash the bundles we threw in, one at a time, and make a huge stack of straw with the residue, the chaff from this bundle. Just to see a large pile or stack of straw, we knew that thrashers had already been there.

At that time, straw would bring about five cents a bale. It wasn't worth the baling cost; it cost three cents to bale at that time. It was interesting as we would compare the costs, even in those days, of what the service would be and what the end product would have to sell for, in order to afford doing it. Straw would not sell for enough to pay for the cost of baling. But in today's market, people will pay even as much as $5 for a bale of straw if they want to decorate for Halloween or for the Fall!

I had a pair of new overalls to start school each fall. Early on, as we loaded all the bundles onto the wagons to take to the thrashing machine, I was so proud of these new overalls that I wore them for thrashing! But these new overalls didn't work, because they were so filled with starch it made them thread-bare by night. So I learned: never wear a pair of new overalls for thrashing. I had to wear my used overalls, maybe even patched, to school the first day because my new ones were already worn out just from thrashing.

We had one of the finest dairy barns in this part of the country at that time. It was up to date with concrete floors and white interior, with the ceiling and the walls all painted white. We cleaned the barn each day: the concrete floor; the troughs where all the feces would be gathered in one trough; put lime on the concrete floor. All these things taught me not only responsibility but dedication to a job. If there was to be play-time, it came second. I adopted that philosophy all throughout my life: work first; play after I get the work done. My grandfa-ther was very good at that.

All these things on the farm taught me most of the values which I still cherish: whatever I make, save some of it; be hon-est, be fair, be ethical in whatever I do; learn to work with and help others.

Even the radio shows taught me. My grandparents would listen to "Amos 'n Andy" every time it was on. We'd sit there glued to our chairs, our eyes staring at the radio as if we could see the person speaking! We learned from Fibber McGee and Molly as they would perform, and as Squire Skimp would run the Jot'em Down Store. They'd get some wild ideas sometimes and then they might open the closet and things would fall out, and we'd think, "Whatever we do, we'll keep our closet clean, our clothes hung up and neat. We sure don't want to have a Fib-ber-McGee-and-Molly closet!"

They were high up in The Lodge, whatever it was. Grand-mother also was very active in Lodge work, in the Masonic order, Eastern Star. And sometimes, when I was very small, she'd be sitting on the front porch watching any traffic that might come by and reciting to herself the memory of this Lodge work, Masonic work that she had to do, and sometimes I'd look at her and scratch my head, and say, "Grandma, who you talkin' to?" and she'd say, "Now, this is some of my Lodge work!" It was a hush-hush type of thing. So I'd go on off and play, because she wasn't talking to me, she was doing her "memory work."

Well, they came home from The Lodge one night in 1929 in their brand-new, four-door Studebaker car, with big round disk wheels, beautiful blue with a black canvas top. Grandfather got out of the car, to open the garage doors. It was not an attached garage as we see today; it was a detached garage away from the house and it was in what we call the barn lot. And as he got out of the car and went to open the garage doors–they were large hinged doors at that time, each had to be propped open, one at a time–this bull, a Jersey bull, got him down and really gored him. My grandmother was able to get a broom and kind of beat the bull off, but it was too late by the time she ran to get a broom. I was not there at the time, but that's probably why I went there to stay because he never really felt good after that and wasn't able to do the farm work himself.

He would be able to sit up in a chair or walk some, but not go out and work behind a plow all day, nothing like that, or never go to the barn to milk. It was mostly from the porch that he gave me directions and taught me.

We had around forty Jersey cows, most of the time. The barn could hold only thirty, so we'd let some of them out and then let the rest of them in. We had Jersey cows because they had more butterfat in their milk, and that's what people thought they wanted in those days,

I was about six years old when they started me out with milking. At that time they had gallon buckets that syrup came in, like molasses. So they started me milking the smaller cows or the cows that were nearly through with their lactation period, and I could hold that gallon bucket between my legs. I milked until I went into the army.

I didn't have the clothing that others had. When I went to

McGregor Elementary School, for those six years, I had only one pair of shoes at a time. Whether I was in the barn or in school, it was the same pair. And then when they about got worn out, then I got a new pair and maybe could use the old ones for the barn exclusively and the new ones to go to school with for a while until the old ones gave out completely.

Of course, I had one pair of overalls, one shirt. My grandmother oftentimes would make flannel shirts for the wintertime, buying flannel goods. Even some of the feed sacks for the dairy farm or for the chickens were out of material that could be recycled into clothing or dresses or shirts.

And even when the clothing wore out, my grandmother had a very unique way of cutting it into strips and weaving braided rugs. She would take the other material and cut them into squares or designs and sew them together into comforters or quilts. They didn't waste anything; they were very thrifty people. All this had an effect on me: to be thrifty in whatever I did. Not only to save some, but use what was available so I didn't waste money buying things I didn't need.

She was the matriarch of the family, after my grandfather got attacked by the bull. She, too, would share with me good work ethic. I never learned to cook, and I didn't want to, she did all the cooking. I would come in from the milking barn and get ready to go to school, and she prepared the lunch I'd take with me. Sometimes it was made with leftover biscuits so I was reluctant to eat in front of other students who had the fancier, store-bought "light bread" for their sandwiches. Other students might have had bologna or lunch meat in their light-bread sandwiches whereas mine would have a pork chop or a slice of ham or sausage, very good meat, but in a homemade biscuit.

Grandmother did the laundry. She had her wash day not particularly on one day each week, but on a day when the weather would permit it. Sometimes the laundry might accumulate for a couple of weeks in the wintertime until a decent day when it wasn't freezing. There was no automatic washer or automatic dryer!

She had a cistern that would catch the rainwater off the roof and this was supposedly soft water as opposed to hard water that was in the well. And so the cistern's soft water was what she used for laundry day. And she had a separate building out from the main house that had her wringer-type washing machine. Oh, Maytag should have been proud of that! We had three tubs and the tubs were filled with this water, and that was my job, on laundry day, to fill the washing machine tubs with water from this cistern because it was soft water.

Some of it we had to put bluing in, little balls of blue, about the size of marbles, and we put that in the water to finish, and the white clothes seemed so white.

And then if the clotheslines were not sufficient to hold everything she'd washed, then we could string clothes on the fence. It was not a barbed wire fence, but a woven wire fence that surrounded the house, to separate it from the garden. I helped her hang the clothes, but it had to be when I was not in school. In the summertime, sometimes the first ones hung on the line would have dried by the time the last ones went on the line, just from the wind.

Then, in between her other chores, she always loved flowers and they were in the garden. It seemed that, planting her flowers in the garden, Grandpa would have to plow in between the rows of the flowers while he was plowing the garden–before his accident.

They'd get Straight Run, a type of baby chicken, and when they grew up, the roosters, the males, were the ones we could process for eating. We always had fried chicken in the spring of the year! After things advanced, then there were locker plants in town, where we would go in and rent locker space, a large drawer, where we could process the chickens and vegetables there, which was some relief to my grandma because she didn't have to do the home canning in the glass jars.

We each took turns killing the chickens to eat. Grandma

was quite handy: she could either take one by the neck and turn it around and around and twist its head off, or she could have us lay the head of the chicken on a chopping block at the woodpile and she'd chop its head off. And then the chicken would jump around like…a chicken with its head cut off! Then we would strip the feathers off, prepare it, process it.

Back then, all of us who grew up on farms learned about processing meat, whether it was pork or beef or chickens. To have link sausage, they would take some of the intestines from the pig and clean them. There wasn't a thing wasted; in fact, Grandmother told me there wasn't a thing wasted but the squeal, on a pig! We processed everything, from pigs' feet to pigs' ears to chitterlings to sausage to hams.

We cured our own, hung them up to cure. It seemed there was always some type of ham processing taking place: Morton-Salt cured or sugar-cured. They had them hanging up in the smoke house, a smaller building, to cure because, again, this was before the days of freezers. The same was true with the bacon and the salt pork. Much of the fat from the hog was stripped off into a large kettle and processed into lard, which would be the equivalent of what we know as shortening today.

My grandmother in the summertime had a card she'd put in the window. It had 25, 50, 75, 100 for pounds, and depending on which way she turned it up, the iceman, as he'd come by, would bring a chunk of ice to our house and put it in the icebox on the back porch. Frequently in the summertime it might be a 100 that she'd turn up so we could take and chip some of the ice off and make ice cream with the home freezer.

All of this was part of living in those days. I'm thankful for that, because that experience alone taught me to appreciate so many new ways of processing what we've always had.

When it came time for me to go to Senior High School, that was a little bit too far to ride the bike. Besides, my grandfather passed away either my freshman or sophomore year, they sold about two dozen of the cows, and I moved into town with my brother and my mother. I stayed two weeks! Maybe just a week! They said, "You better come on back," so I returned to the farm.

My uncle took care of my grandmother, after my grandfather died. She was kind of a large woman. My uncle's house was sixty acres south of us, and he would come there each day. Grandmother never learned to drive a car. Matter of fact, she learned to drive a team when she was young, but never after that did she drive a team or drive a car.

At Grandma's, I had my own room. It was a large two-story home, and it had hot water heat with radiators, so it was always warm in the wintertime. And if I needed some of my clothes laundered, I could wash them myself and lay them on the radiators and that would dry them. I rode a bicycle from the farm at what is now the corner of the Horton Smith Golf Course, at Golden and West Seminole–today's street names–to Springfield Senior High at the corner of Central and Jefferson Streets, about six miles from home. Now it's called Central High School.

When I was in high school I wasn't thinking about preparing for college, because WWII came on and my father persuaded me to go with him to Seattle, Washington, where some of his family lived. He was going to work in the shipyards for the war effort, and I would go to school.

My dad's name was O.D., which stood for Oren Dewey. Because he did not like that name, everyone called him Jack and he went by the name of Jack Manley all his life. After my mother and dad were divorced, oftentimes he would leave here and go to Seattle, then come back after a year or two. He did not have a high school education, and certainly no college, and he was a plumber by trade; my grandfather Manley taught my dad the plumbing and heating business.

Sometimes Dad would go to where the jobs were. Coming through a Depression, there wasn't a lot of hot water heating with radiators taking place here in Springfield, so he decided to move to Seattle, a much larger town that was gearing up for war.

I went at his insistence and for one year, from 1939 to 1940,

I went to high school in Seattle, Washington. But I liked the farm, Seattle was town living, and it rained too much for me.

We were living with his mother, my grandmother, in a little two-story house in the city. I still remember the address: 6939 Fauntleroy. Much of the crowd that my dad was with, including his sisters and brothers, were pretty well-to-do. Betty Manley Evans's husband, Harry Evans, was a metallurgist and had quite a good job as an executive with Boeing Aircraft. It was just coming into big existence. Bess Manley Sullivan's husband, Leonard, was a tile setter, and was setting tile everywhere–tile on the walls and floors, ceramic tile. Dad's brother Ed Manley also did all kinds of tile work. His brother Earl had lived in Seattle, but entered the military service even during the Depression years and I don't know what happened to him; I saw him one time. Dad's sister Opal Manley Dickens lived there also.

All three of those sisters of his served overseas as nurses during WWI. And in those days a nurse was scarce, hard to come by. I don't know if they had all the training that they have today, but they certainly had some formal training, I do know that.

The Manley Family-Eddie, Bessie, Betty, Opal

They were very proud. And they all had families of their own.

My grandmother wanted to play cards all the time; that's the first time I ever learned to play Pitch and Pinochle. But I didn't like that either.

My father played golf. And so did his twin sisters, Betty and Bess. I did caddie at the Lakewood Golf Course where he played regularly, particularly weekends, with my uncles, his sisters' husbands; they all played golf too. So I would caddie on weekends, then, to have a little spending money of my own.

At that time, yellow corduroy pants was the vogue and fashion in Seattle! But what was really the "in" thing, and I hated it, was who could have the dirtiest, most torn yellow cord pants with the most white athletic tape mending the tears. I did not participate in that! I just could not accept it.

It was kind of an adventure for me to go there, because I don't think I'd been out of the city of Springfield! Maybe to Nixa or Ozark. To go that far! But once I was there, I was not happy.

According to those people at the school, though I did not know it, I spoke with a southern drawl. Some of them would kid me, the way I talked. They spoke more like a Little Lord Fauntleroy, faster, with a more distinct type English, like the British or a person from Boston or the East might speak. And I didn't like that either.

At the time there was a movie going on, and I don't remember anything about it because I didn't go, I didn't have money for a movie, but, the name of it was *Hell's A Poppin'*. So I wrote my mother a letter and said, "Hell's a poppin', I'd rather come home." So my mother sent me money to come home, and I came back to Springfield Senior High–SHS.

I had to take Math and English but they were not my fondest subjects. History was okay. My grandmother wanted me to take Latin and be a lawyer. I took a course in Latin and I didn't like that at all! Latin was dead, as far as I was concerned, so I said, "I'll never be a lawyer!"

Then I went to the military service my senior year. Both Roland and I got credit for being in the service, we just had half a year to go in school; many young men and women did that. It was the patriotic thing to do!

I was not there to graduate with them, and, in my case, I still had gone to the farm each day: I didn't have time for extra-curricular activities. Today, I recognize many of the names, but I'm not close to my high school classmates. I had been a bashful boy who never got away from home much. I was a country boy and I was going to a city school; I was living with my grandparents on the dairy farm. I was bashful to the extent I felt a little bit "underneath" other students, because they had maybe two or three pair of shoes and several changes of clothes. I had one pair of shoes and probably no more than two changes of clothes.

There weren't many cars around. On extremely bad days, my uncle would try to take me–even though I might be a little late, rather than make two trips–because they took the milk from the dairy farm to the creamery each morning. He would go home to his house and eat breakfast, then come back and load the milk on the truck and take it to the creamery.

They had an interest in a creamery in town, Tracy Creamery Company, on Main Street just north of Walnut. We would go there to take milk, and there was occasion– when my uncle for whatever reason was either ill or out of town showing his bird dogs or show horses–that I would have to take the milk to town, and he taught me where the freezer was at that Tracy Creamery Company. They made all kinds of ice cream and popsicles. To go there and get three or four popsicles! I mean, this was like going to a county fair, a great experience! I looked forward to taking the milk to town because I was going to get some popsicles and ice cream!

During the war, they'd done without gas, without trucks and cars, had to patch tires and tubes, because the military service took much of those things, and with rationing on, they had to have special reasons. I guess the farms had a priority to get certain things, I don't know, I believe they did. My grandparents were able to continue the farming.

After the war, I came back and Grandma had, of course, been a widow for some time. She never had a wheel chair or anything like that, but she would get around with a cane, when she got older.

My uncle and a part-time farm hand kept it going. It was very difficult to keep a farm hand in those days. The one that they had, Charley Myers, had to go to the military service. They'd get someone to help for only a few months at a time or maybe just the summertime. My uncle had to do it with whatever help he could get.

After I got home from the service and then while I went to Drury, I could help on Saturdays when they had the heavier work to do, like building fences and driving posts that they could not do while I was gone. Because of the war, I was a picture of health, lots of muscles, so digging post holes didn't pose a problem. In many cases they didn't have the steel posts that we know today, because that all had gone to war, but they had about a 20-acre tract that was all timber. We could cut a tree with a cross-cut saw–that would be two of us sawing a small tree–then split and sharpen it with an ax. It was easy to sharpen the green wood with an ax, and then we could drive that fence post into the ground, particularly in the wintertime, but not in the summertime.

So I'd help some with that as I went to college, but basically it weaned me from the farm after the military service. Because my uncle couldn't see after everything himself, they had already cut to the number of cows that he could handle, and milk by hand, and still take the milk.

I don't know how my mother and my dad met. He was from here. After his father and mother divorced, his three sisters and two brothers went to Seattle with their mother. Why? I don't know. In those days divorce was probably looked upon quite differently than it is today. My grandmother was Molly Cain Manley.

Grandfather stayed here because of the property. His name was C.C. Todd Manley. He didn't like C.C.–it stood for Charles something–so they called him Todd.

He was in the plumbing and heating business here in Springfield for many many years. He retired just after the Depression from Manley Plumbing and Heating. They did a lot of hot water heating and a lot of steam heating. The city of Springfield, at one time, had a steam plant here, through the downtown area, with steam pipes, and when radiators were put in the buildings, the steam would heat them. Of course, that failed just like the horse and buggy. But hot water heating with radiators was quite their specialty at that time and that was what they installed, for the most part. It was not furnaces as we know today.

Today we have forced air furnaces, by natural gas. In those days, they'd heat water, and they had a boiler rather than a furnace in each home, and only the luxury homes had those. Even hospitals at that time had that type of heat, not only because it was the most economical but also because it was the most healthy.

A number of my homes that I built in earlier years had baseboard heating, which would be hot water pumped by a boiler through baseboard heating around the edge of a home, so it was easy to maintain the same temperature, and there wasn't the dust or pollution that might occur from a forced air furnace that now blows heat out from the furnace pipes in the floor and the ceiling.

I did not know Grandfather Manley well; he was kind of gruff. He had a big nose that reminded me of a strawberry. Earlier, he was quite one with truck gardening, besides his plumbing and heating business, and had large strawberry patches. He'd get students to come out and pick a quart of strawberries at two to three cents a box, during the season. He was quite noted for raising good strawberries around here. I remember the carrier with the handle on it, and there could be eight boxes there in this carrier. He'd have all those stored in a special shed on the farm, about twenty acres all together, and some of that today is where Kansas Expressway goes across. The land is still there. Of course, he had long since sold it.

"My paternal grandfather, Charles C. 'Todd' Manley (far left)"

Grandfather Manley never remarried. He stayed here, died with a small home and some acreage and a car, all paid for, but that was about it. During the Depression years he had sort of whittled away any wealth; he had been relatively wealthy.

Some of my classmates from McGregor School would go there and pick strawberries and what a time that was! They had quite a selection of penny candy at Conine's Grocery Store across from the school. They couldn't go there during school hours, but they could before school and after school.

I didn't live with my mother very much because the farm was just less stress and trouble for me. I wanted those chores. And my grandparents would have meals every day, and my mother oftentimes, by herself, was not at home to cook because she was working. War made women leave the home and go to work because of the shortage of people. I stayed with the farm until they sold it, after the war and after they quit the dairy business.

Grandma Kreider, my mother's mother, was much more to my life than my parents were. My mother wasn't jealous of that. She was grateful. They were close.

My mother was a good worker and a loving mother. She loved her children but she had to work. In those days I don't think they had the child support laws they have today; to my knowledge my father didn't pay very much child support, if any, but he would help along as he was paid for various large jobs; it was during the Depression years and I'm sure much of his work was on commission. My grandparents would supplement with farm products, whether it was flour or fruits or vegetables that they raised on the farm. Oftentimes my grandmother would have my uncle to stop by my mother's house in town, in Springfield, on the way to the creamery and leave a gallon of milk for her at her house, because my sister and my brother lived with her. That helped a lot.

Mother worked at Martin Brothers Piano Company in town for a number of years, selling pianos and appliances, as a means of income. My grandparents bought this home for her where she lived as well as deeding my uncle this sixty-acre farm with a house on it. So they helped their kids to have their homes, and certainly my mother was very grateful for that. It was not what we'd call a thermostating home because it was still one that had to be heated with a wooden stove. But she did have a gas cook range, because in town there was natural gas available. That made it easier.

As my brother and sister got older, they continued to live with my mother and they worked some at grocery stores, stocking shelves and carrying out groceries.

On Sundays or weekends, we might start the fire up–there were two stoves, one in the living room and one in the combination kitchen-bedroom–and one chimney served all of it. Even today, when I go out 60 Highway East and pass where some of the Amish live, Seymour and that area, I see the large two-story homes and a chimney on each end. Occasionally there might be one with a chimney in the middle but it probably would be a single-family home rather than a two-family home.

After the war I was a man, I had seen the world, I wanted a home of my own, I wanted to get married, raise a family. Because of the GI Bill, I wanted an education. I went to college, in less than four years, because I went in the summertime, too. I wanted to get through. I learned a lot in college as far as business was concerned, then called Economics. They didn't yet offer Building as a major. That's when I got the background for the very business that I went in all the rest of my life.

My dad was probably 78 to 80 when he died. It was with a heart problem. He died here in town, in the hospital, and he didn't really like to go the hospital. In my dad's time, if someone went to the hospital, he went there to die. Nowadays we go there to be treated for our health problems, not to die. He didn't like it when we put him in the hospital, but it was some type of heart failure.

How am I like my father? That's a good question. My father and I were never close. I never spent time with my dad. I lived with my grandparents and what I learned as a child from home would be from my grandparents. Of course, they taught me thrift; they taught me work ethic; they taught me whatever I made, save some of it; honesty; if I want something, work for it. That type philosophy. Very good people!

My father was one that, if he saw a problem, he might walk off and leave it. He went from here to Seattle a number of

"My father, Oren Dewey 'Jack' Manley, 58 years old (born May 30, 1898)"

times, when things didn't go to suit him here, particularly after he and my mother divorced, when I was just a young boy. He did not have much stability. When he got to about fifth grade, he began helping his dad in the plumbing and heating business. He didn't understand financing and ownership. He never owned a piece of property and he never saved very much, he just spent what he made.

My grandparents thought my father, by playing golf so much, put golf ahead of work. He played golf, if not every day, then every other day. He was quite a golfer, was a par shooter in his earlier years. Of course, there were three of us children, and he might have let some of the family needs go, in order to play golf, and my grandparents didn't like that at all. So I'd have to say, my grandparents were not really fond of him…but he did put hot water heat in their big two-story house! And he added indoor plumbing, too; they had not had indoor plumbing previously.

Dad played golf at different golf courses. Actually, where the

U.S. Medical Center is now, here in Springfield, was Lakeshore Country Club. And, then, it had two golf courses: three or four hundred acres, half a section of land. But it fell into disrepair during the Depressions years, so the city bought it and gave it to the Federal Government to build the U.S. Medical Center, at Sunshine and Kansas Expressway.

He'd work some, he'd play some. He was not a saver; he was a spender. He also played at a country club on Glenstone where Evangel College is now. That country club also went into default during the Depression years, so the city bought it for the federal government to build what was then O'Reilly General Hospital for the Veterans, during WWII times. The only building left from the hospital is the Administration Building, and I think they're building a new one. All the rest have been torn down and replaced with other buildings.

He was a good worker and I admired my father in a number of ways because he was my father. But I didn't want to pattern after him. He married a couple of times, after my mother and he divorced, after a number of years. None of the marriages did well and I think he divorced them all, and ended up before his death as a single person, living in the little home here in Springfield that I bought for him and furnished, rather than have him live with me while I was raising our family, because we did have different ideas about things and it would not have worked for us to live together, and I knew that. I did not want to be like him because I wanted to raise a family; I wanted to have savings; I wanted to buy real estate; all these things. It was quite different.

What I learned from my father was what not to do, and from my grandparents who raised me, what to do.

I don't know any more on my father's side, because my grandparents raised me and that's why I know all this; I lived there on the land where I live now.

My sister, Dorothy Manley, was two years older. There was two years' difference between my sisters: Mary Louise would have been four years older than me; my sister Dorothy two years older; my brother and I, the youngest.

Dorothy had joined the WACs. It was the patriotic thing to do for all young people–of age, of course–to join the military service. The Women's Army Corp was the first one for women.

Dorothy was attached to the Air Force. She had basic training as far as marching, but not for weapons. She was doing office work, secretarial-type work in the Air Force. She was based at Truex Field, Wisconsin, at an air base and may have gone to other bases, but certainly not overseas, always in the United States, and always attached to the Air Force.

The Army Air Corp and the Army was one and the same. It was only after the war that they separated the two, and the Air Force became a separate unit with different uniforms than the Army and the Army uniforms.

Probably one of the things that brought that about: the British had them separated, and the British uniforms were light blue and very pretty uniforms. Of course, the Army uniforms were the olive drab, and certainly that was not an appropriate color for the Air Force as they would go into the "wild blue yonder." So they changed after the war, and they made the Air Force uniforms blue.

My sister didn't choose to go into the Air Force; they took their skills and she had typing, maybe shorthand, in school because that was the thing for a woman to do in high school in that day. We had not started to college yet because there was not a chance to, so she had those skills and so the decision was cut and dry. Women did not go to combat units or infantry units; they went to desk jobs.

After the war Dorothy went to college with me, graduated from Drury College here in Springfield. The colleges were jammed with veterans because the Veterans' Administration paid their tuition and bought their books.

Dorothy Francis Manley met and married Charles Turner. She might have known her husband before college, but not on

"My wife Jayne, me at 28, and my 30-year-old sister,
Dorothy Manley Turner, in 1951"

a dating basis. He was a Cumberland Presbyterian Minister, eventually, and they both had attended a Cumberland Presbyterian Church, so they knew each other from there. I think Dorothy's major in college was sociology and a lot of psychology because this is what her husband did. Of course she had the basics of secretarial work as well.

After the war and college she went to work for the FAA, Federal Aviation Administration, and worked there for many years. She and her husband did not have any children but they adopted two daughters. When they got the notice to adopt one, within a day or two they got the other notice, so they just adopted them both and reared them. The daughters, my nieces, are living in Oklahoma City now; we do not have close ties.

With my sister we did; we'd go and visit. As a minister, I think Charles started out in Tennessee, and we'd go down to Tennessee and visit them, and then Oklahoma.

They both are deceased and both are buried in Oklahoma

City, Oklahoma. Dorothy passed away about four or five years ago, in Oklahoma. My mother, later on, lived in Arizona, and then Oklahoma City.

My sister and her two adopted girls inherited my mother's assets and my sister's assets. I never inherited one cent. Not one cent. I gave rather than received.

The Manley Cemetery down here on Wilson's Creek near James River in southwest Greene County, into Christian County, that's my relatives. My father and others of the Manley family are buried there. I do not desire to be buried there, because that was not my home. It was part of the Manley home. Many of them lived there, some on the battlefield site. As a young boy I met them, but I didn't know them very well. I have no idea when they may have passed away, or any heirs or property. But I do know my dad is buried there, two of my dad's brothers are buried there, and my dad's father–my grandfather Manley–is buried there.

I send a contribution there each year for the cemetery upkeep, and I think they purchased some more land there. Frankly, I don't go there very often, not even every year.

I do go to my mother's grave. She's buried in the Kreider plot out here in Hazelwood Cemetery, here in Springfield, where the Kreiders are buried.

I have a separate cemetery plot; it too is in Hazelwood, but it's a full block with twelve plots, and a large tombstone is there but no graves. It already says Manley; it's as big as this desk. I tell the story to some of the people that it was my wife's birthday last year when we bought that, so she said, "What are you going to get me for this year?" and I said "Nothing, because you didn't use what I got you last year!"

Now that didn't actually happen, no it didn't; I just tell it because it promotes laughter and I love laughter!

Part 5

Personal Life: Wife, Daughters, Grandsons, Leisure Activities, and Favorite Foods

When I met her down there, at Taylor's, I was a veteran who wanted a home, somebody to share it with, somebody I could talk with. We hit it off.

Immediate Family

My wife is Jayne Marian, an Atteberry girl from a little town called Charity–the natives called it Hog Eye, I'm not sure why. Charity is about thirty miles north of Springfield, Missouri, and east of Buffalo.

Charity had a little general store where a person could buy anything from cow feed to hay to groceries: a small general store for a small community. Jayne's father ran it originally, but it closed during the Depression years.

Then her brother, Duane Atteberry, set up another one there later on. He had a stock truck in which he'd bring livestock to Springfield for his customers, unload them at the yards, then haul back the groceries and feed that he needed for his store in Charity. I'm sure he had to wash it!

While a student at Drury, I'd leave the college to go and get a sandwich or snack at Taylor's Drive-In by the American Legion Home, on the corner of Benton and Trafficway–and there she was, working, waiting tables. Jayne and her sister Joella lived in an apartment here in town and both worked at restaurant jobs.

When I met her down there, at Taylor's, I was a veteran who wanted a home, somebody to share it with, somebody I could

"Jayne and Joella Atteberry in 1949."

talk with. We hit it off. I graduated from Drury College in 1949. We got married April 30, 1950, in Harrison, Arkansas.

"Our wedding chapel in Harrison, Arkansas, April 30, 1950, and honeymoon car."

Several years later my wife was pregnant with our first child, and we were building our home on five acres my grandmother had given me across from her home, what is now West Seminole Street. I had begun building homes, twenty houses on twenty acres in the first subdivision I developed, in Fairmont Acres.

I had bought in trade the balance of that tract, fifteen acres, from my mother, trading a new car for her land.

We had the garage finished first, so we moved into it from an apartment. My wife helped me to put on the lathing for the plaster, typical in those days, with a carpenter's apron on. Of course, being pregnant, the carpenter's apron was almost lying out flat where the nails would fall out!

In building this first home, we stacked up boards–about eight-foot-tall, one-by-twelve boards–in about a three-foot square, and that was our outhouse, temporarily, until we got the house built. As a joke, I took my keyhole saw and sawed a round circle in the board that we'd go through to get into the outhouse so she could go in sideways, because she was pregnant.

I was also building a house next door. The house was bricked up only about halfway on the front, it wasn't finished yet, so on September 23, 1953, when the baby was born, I took and painted, in large letters with a paintbrush, "It's a girl!"

"Janell Kay Manley, our first child!"

Janell Kay: our first child! We had three altogether, about two years apart, and all three are daughters: Jodell Sue was born May 22, 1955, and Jennifer Lee was born March 10, 1958. My wife was from a family of ten children. Seven of those children were girls. All those girls' names began with J and the middle name began with M. That gave her the idea she would name our daughters with the J and M, the M being Manley. All of my wife's sisters did the same thing with their children, except one sister who named her daughter Valerie.

One of my workers brought me a young rooster. This rooster turned out to be a pet and followed me to the job or wherever. When Janell was born, this rooster resented me carrying her or looking after her, and would want to peck her, because I wasn't petting him. So rather than have that rooster by himself, I built a little shed and bought some chickens to go with that rooster, a dozen female chickens, so he would not be lonesome or chase my girls anymore!

"My dad, Jack Manley, holding Jodell; Jayne in the middle;
I'm holding Janell. January 1956."

When the middle daughter, Jodell, was born, we were in another house. Sometimes if we were living in one of the homes in this subdivision and somebody wanted that house rather than the house we were building, we would move and let them buy ours. We did that four or five times. Then as we accumulated financial strength, we didn't want to do that anymore.

We always had a very nice home because a builder should: people would come in, see, and decide on our quality of workmanship. When all three of the girls had arrived, we lived on Manley Drive, the only street in this first subdivision. This was an acre lot, and I built a cute little shed there, with a white, wood, ranch-type fence around it.

We had the chickens, and Jayne's father, Orval Atteberry, gave us some Bantam eggs and some duck eggs, so when one of the chickens went to setting, we put some of these Bantam eggs and duck eggs under that chicken. When they hatched, the little ducks would get in the water trough and the mother hen would just get so frustrated! She couldn't understand those baby ducks getting in the water tank. Baby Bantams of course couldn't; they would have drowned.

Later on, as the girls were older, we bought more acreage on the farm and hadn't developed it yet–into another subdivision called Camelot–so the girls learned about the facts of life. We had cows with baby calves; sheep with baby lambs; chickens with babies; baby ducks. They saw the chickens hatch and the sheep as they would breed and then have the baby lambs. It was a great opportunity for me, a man, to be able to talk with them in such a way that they understood.

We even bought a pony and Jodell, the middle daughter, was very proficient, very early, at driving that pony up and

"Janell, Jodell, and Jennifer Manley"

"The Manley Family in the early 1960's"

down the street (where we didn't want her to go), with all the lines and harness attached to the pony, while riding in the little cart behind.

We even used that little cart as a sleigh. I would sit on it; there were no runners; it was just strictly at Christmas, painted all up like a Santa Claus sleigh, and we would deliver Christmas gifts to people who had bought houses from us that year, and Jodell would drive! We kept that for several years. The children loved it.

They were proud. A lot of neighbor kids would come to our house because we had all the animals and the pony and the lambs.

And I made them a little doll house. As a builder, of course I had to.

I'm happy for the life we've had, happy for the opportunity to raise our children where they could learn all the things I call Biology Lessons: the animals being born, how they were born, and the gestation periods. Gosh, they could all tell you it takes twenty-one days for a chicken to hatch but it takes nine months for a calf to be born and it takes eleven months for a colt to be born. We've had all of those!

One of the sheep had three lambs one time, and the girls called them Peter, Paul, and Mary, because that was one of the singing groups in that day. Well, one lamb was hanging halfway out of the mama, so I pulled that lamb out of the mama, with the girls watching, and we wrapped it up in an old towel and put it in a box near the fireplace in our home. That lamb survived and was a great pet. These girls would rock that lamb as if it were a baby doll and that lamb loved it. I don't know if it was Peter, Paul, or Mary but the girls would know. When people would come to the house, some of the sales people or people who were interested in buying a house from us, the girls would yell and that lamb would run for the voice of those girls. It was quite a happy time.

Our girls never gave us any trouble. They realized the facts of life in such a way that it made a lasting impression on them. They were really well prepared, as they advanced in age, to handle all those things that come up in a young person's life. It was great training for them.

They had a little dog, a French poodle, named Pierre. People we built a house for gave us that little dog. Those girls would treat Pierre like a baby also, even fix it sometimes with a little hat or a dress. It was so humorous.

If boys would come to the house or in the house, if they even got close to the girls, Pierre would go and nip them on the ankles. That dog saw that nobody was near those girls, nobody was going to hurt them! Even if I would just play, get rough, say, "I'm gonna get you!" it would get on me! It was a great protector!

One time we had a cat named Thumbelina, and somehow or other it got caught in the garage door, and when the garage door came down, it pinched that cat between the door and the jam. We didn't know it had been on top of the garage door. So we had to have a little burial for Thumbelina.

Janell, after college graduation, went to work for Commerce Bank here in town, and then from there she went to Southwestern Bell in St. Louis. Her job was to invest reserve funds that Southwestern Bell had by buying shopping centers and other properties. She did very well and learned a lot about real estate and real estate investments.

Janell has never married. She does have three cats. They are her children! She babies and pampers those cats. The one she started with, died. She cried and we had to have a funeral, as we did when the girls were young. If one of the pets died, we'd have a little funeral. One of them would say a prayer, and we would bury the cat or kitten or whatever.

"Jayne, Ruffles, me, and my 1985 Chevrolet truck"

Janell had a dog she got at the pound; it was part beagle and part something else. She named him Ruffles. In St. Louis, she'd leave that dog during the day at home, a two-story with a basement, and it chewed all the spindles on her stairway. I think it did even more damage! Finally she said, "I've got to get rid of this dog. Will you keep it for me?"

We kept Ruffles for about fifteen years and then we finally had the veterinarian put it to sleep. We buried Ruffles in a special way. Whenever we had wanted to go someplace and we'd get a suitcase out, that dog would want to get in that suitcase; it wanted to go, too. So we buried Ruffles in one of those very suitcases in the backyard. Jayne and I both shed a few tears. The tombstone in the backyard says, "Ruffles, Family Dog, Born (such and such), Died (such and such)."

Then the real babies came along: our grandchildren.

After Jennifer, the youngest, graduated from college, she went to work with Southwestern Bell in St. Louis. She met Skip Davis, from Chetopa, Kansas, married him, and worked there for a few years.

"Jennifer Manley Davis, 46; Skip Davis, 48; their sons, Jeffrey Michael, 18; Jared Marshall and Jason Matthew, the twins, 15, in November, 2004."

"Jennifer and Skip's sons around 1995."

Their first child, our first grandchild, was a boy, Jeff. We'd go back and forth to St. Louis to visit them. Then Jennifer called all excited that she was going to have another baby, but it wasn't just one baby: it was twins! She said she did not want to stay there and raise twins by herself. So when it got closer to her time, they moved back to Springfield. Janell, who also had moved to St. Louis, didn't want to stay there by herself so she also came back to Springfield. We helped Jennifer with the twins.

As we managed our business from home, our three daughters would hear me talking with people all the time. People would come to the house because we designed as well as built homes. So the girls were exposed at home to all the aspects of real estate and the home-building industry.

When Jennifer, Skip, and Janell moved back to Springfield, that's when we got each of them interested in the business. Skip, at the time, couldn't build. He was quite a computer operator, but we introduced him to the business, too.

Janell Manley has been building for years now, and has her own subdivisions, the last one being Diamond Park Subdivision. And then she built a lot of patio homes–duplexes that she could sell half of, because they had a zero lot line–in what they

call Fox Grape Subdivision. Beautiful homes. She's done well in the building business and done some duplexes not very far from this office here, south of Battlefield Road, on Fort Street. She too had a good education. She received her Master's in Business Administration at Drury College.

Jennifer Manley Davis builds and develops real estate. Skip and Jennifer work together, and Jennifer is my secretary here. She works flex time, in that she gets her boys off to

"Janell Manley"

school and then she comes and works, and then she picks them up at school; she leaves here in time to do that. Flex time, for me, works perfectly, because I don't really need a secretary eight hours a day.

Jennifer and I manage Ralph K. Manley and Co., our real estate business. I have a number of real estate investments. We rent, sell, and finance. She takes care of calculating the payment, insurance, and taxes; everything is computerized and she's my computer expert.

Jodell was not interested in the building business; she wanted to teach. Then she got her master's degree in counseling, which she loves. Jodell's first marriage ended in divorce. Then she married another fellow, and their baby, the fourth of

"Jodell and Jordan, 1995."   "Jodell and Jordan, 2002."

our grandsons, was born premature. Jordan was so small that he weighed a pound and a half, and I held him in one hand.

I gave several blood transfusions so that he could make it; to this day I still give blood transfusions and they call it Baby Quad, because they can get four transfusions to babies from the blood that I have. It's type O negative, and somehow it's good for babies.

Jordan was so tiny, he was in St. John's Hospital for quite some time. The staff really nurtured him. Jodell's husband at that time was in the sign business; some were along the highway. Well, he put up a billboard that said, "Thank you, St. John's!" and had a picture of the baby there.

Jodell divorced Jordan's father, her second divorce, and because there were no boys to carry on the name of Manley, she gave Jordan the last name of Manley rather than the name of his father, her husband at that time Jordan was born.

Jordan's fine and well today. He's still young enough he likes Grandma to be around, to take him shopping. The other boys, of course, would be embarrassed if their Grandma had to take them to school, but Jordan still goes for that.

They all live here in town, and we're all very proud of them. We get together on family occasions like Thanksgiving or Christmas, things like that. We're a close-knit family, and get to enjoy our grandchildren.

Jayne and I have a dog now. Its name is Sizzle. Jodell had seen this miniature French poodle mix that had been hit by a car and was injured. She picked it up and took it to the vet and had it brought back to life. She found out a couple of weeks later that she was allergic to dogs so she said, "Would you keep this dog for us?" So we kept it, and now we've had it for several years! Jordan still calls it his dog, "but you're keeping it for me, Grandma and Grandpa."

The other dog we had before him, Ruffles, makes three dogs that we've had in our married life. Pierre, the mid-sized French poodle that the people gave us, that's the one that looked after the children.

The animals have been an important part of the family, because feeding and caring for them each day helped teach our children responsibility, and they're all very responsible. My grandparents taught me responsibility! We have no problem with that; that's just one of those traits we passed on to our children!

And all our daughters have college educations, good education, and that's the key, really, to success in life. And managing people. And managing money.

My family has been a real joy to me: to see them grow; to see them prosper. Each of them has her own profession. I did not ask my girls to go into the real estate business; they chose that, two of them, on their own, and have been very successful with it. I am happy and proud of them all.

Of course, real estate is finance-intensive; it takes a lot of capital to buy lots and build houses. So as we accumulated capital, we were able to build one house, two houses, three houses, four houses, five houses at a time. With raising kids, we always had the braces for the teeth, the clothing.

Because I was not from a wealthy background, just to be able to have a change of clothes was something, without having to wash them and put them back on the next morning!

I appreciate opportunities; I appreciate good health; I appreciate the ability to have a free nation and a free people, to choose my own vocation, and to raise a family.

Leisure Activities

What my family and I have done for fun has changed over the years. We always took small vacations; we had station wagons when the girls were young, six-to-nine-seat passenger station wagons. I remember Ford Country Squires, for example; very beautiful station wagons that could also serve, dual purpose, in my business as far as taking people to show them houses. We took nice vacations, whether it was to Disneyland or Knott's Berry Farm or Six Flags Over Texas. One vacation a year.

"Me, on family vacations at the ocean, in 1987 and parasailing in or about 1998."

I love to snow ski. I started doing that about twenty-five years ago when I was a teacher at SMS. They would have special rates to go snow skiing or other activities during Spring Break, so I went on one of those as a chaperone one time, on the bus. That's when I learned, and I've been snow skiing ever since. Last year we took the whole family snow skiing.

"Left to right: Me, Perry Oberle, Jennifer Manley Davis, Jodell Manley, Jeffrey Davis, Jack Steiger, Skip Davis, in 1989."

And I like to water ski. We keep a boat at a condominium we own down at Table Rock Lake, in Kimberling City, Missouri. We've have it for twenty years. It's kind of a getaway. There's a swimming pool.

I've never been one to fish much. I like to hunt. I like to walk through the woods.

I have a farm at Norwood, Missouri, because I had gone turkey and deer hunting down in Douglas County one time with a friend who had invited me along, a fellow by the name of Cordell Bixler; I call him Bix. We slept in an old abandoned home. They had all kinds of bunk beds. There was no electricity in the place; we had candles and an old wood stove to heat. I didn't get a deer that year but it was fun, exciting, to be deer hunting. There were about eight or ten people there; one was the designated cook, so he'd cook us breakfast and then we'd go out to our various stands.

I enjoyed that so much that, when one of the properties down there became available for sale, this fellow on the 500 acres was not in very good health and his wife was more or less confined to a wheel chair, and this fellow said, "Would you like to buy this place?" and we kind of agreed on the terms of that and shook hands. So I bought it from him, about twenty years ago.

The first year I had it, his wife died, and he did too! His son inherited the mortgage, so I paid his son off, and I did it in three years. I bought another adjoining sixty acres from a fellow that was a drunkard and said he'd like to have another good drunk before he died! I bought that sixty acres from him and within six months he died! And then another adjoining eighty acres became available, so I bought them. Now, collectively, I have 640 acres at Norwood, Missouri, in Douglas County.

"In 1982 I went with some friends on a pheasant hunt in Iowa."

Some of my colleagues, there'll be a dozen or so of us get there during season, and we'll hunt and we'll cook and eat and shoot the breeze and watch video tapes and films, hunting films, and just have a great getaway. But I didn't do this with my daughters.

"A beautiful aerial view of my hunting lodge in Norwood, Missouri."

My daughters do go down there now with their boys, on occasions like during Spring Break, and ride four-wheelers all through the woods, and they enjoy it.

I like cattle. I've had cattle all my life. Growing up, on the farm, I didn't own any; my grandparents did. But when I bought land for future development, we'd run cattle on it and they would keep it clean and we didn't have to mow it. We even had a few sheep, and those sheep would eat the dandelions and the bark off of buck brush and we had the slickest looking farms and fence rows you could imagine! I managed the cattle and the sheep myself. When we were ready to begin developing, we'd move them to another field or another farm.

I have a herd of Angus cattle down at Norwood, about sixty head. I have had as many as a hundred. I don't really want that many down there, because there are certain portions of that farm I don't allow the cattle to run; I want to save that for hunting purposes. The cattle keep the sprouts down, the weeds down. We do mow several of the vacant fields for hay purposes, and have the big round bales of hay to feed the cattle in the wintertime.

Really, it's a hunting lodge, not a farm. I call it a farm but I don't farm. I do have a number of barns, and I've built new barns along and demolished the old ones. The house is decent. At the time I bought it, it was about ten years old. No one lives there permanently.

Cordell Bixler goes down two or three times a week and feeds the cows big round bales, if needed. We have tractors with the spikes on them, to move the bales around the fields, and stock tanks to water them, and ponds. We try to keep the cattle away from the ponds in the wintertime because we did have an occasion when a couple of calves walked out on an ice-frozen pond and broke in, and they drowned, so we said we won't do that anymore. We have stock tanks, with heaters when it's very cold, and of course large loafing sheds for the livestock to get in out of the weather. It works fine.

There are coyotes, coon, bobcat, possum, that are hard on turkey eggs, but we try to eliminate some of those if we can. One year we were driving, Bixler and I, out on one of the open fields, and we saw a coyote running. We tried to run it down with the car, circling around, and it was close enough that I think the coyote was getting tired, so I jumped out of there and stomped that coyote to death! And he's never forgotten that! Cordell always makes fun of that, brings it up, when we're down there.

I try to get there once every week or so, usually on Fridays; Bix and I go down together, then come back that evening. Sometimes I spend the night there. It's completely furnished with everything you can imagine. It's decorated with all kinds of animals.

Cordell is still one of my main hunting buddies, along with his family: his three brothers have three sons; in addition, some friends of each of them come along, so there's usually ten to twelve people there. We have quite a time.

One year it was very cold and rainy. And I don't like to sit in the rain. So I built some outhouses–I'd learn to do that on the farm in early years–about four by four, plus the roof makes it seven feet tall, so we can stand up in them. They have windows on three sides and a door in the back.

We can open the door and set a lawn chair in there, and the windows are such that we can slide the window open and rest a gun barrel on the sill of the window and shoot the deer or turkey without even leaving it. So we really hunt luxuriously. We have little LP gas heaters in there, little battery-operated radios; matter of fact, two of them have battery-operated TV-radios in them, which can be turned down low or used with ear plugs. Then we can sit there and wait in the warm whether it's raining or snowing or whatever.

To hunt, we have one person in each shed. I do have plywood board in each of them, where two could sit there, as one of the hunters may want to teach one of his young sons about hunting. Then the camouflage tents came in, from, like Bass Pro Shop, they're about four feet square and about seven feet tall and have windows on three sides that can zip open, so I have a number of those around that we put up just before each season so we don't sit in the rain. We have little heaters in them, when we need them, and the lawn chairs to sit in. We like to hunt in comfort!

We always kill turkeys. There's lots of game there. Maybe not everybody will get a turkey but most will get a turkey or a deer, and some may get another the second week. We go for two weeks. It's mostly Cordell Bixler and his brothers and his nephews.

I do not smoke; I do not drink; I wouldn't know what-on-earth about drugs, I do not use those in any way, shape, or fashion; I go to bed early and I get up early, and I try to treat my body well. My grandparents taught me, and also college courses, that if I don't feel well, I don't produce well. So if I want to produce the best and get the most from life, I need to keep my body in good shape.

When I first started building, a builder was a carpenter, and I did much of the work myself. Height does not bother me. I was used to heights, climbing up, getting on a roof to put on the rafters or the ceiling joists, or to the second story of a home. Quite a ways off the ground! Construction itself is relatively dangerous: working on uneven ground or off the ground from eight to twenty feet. I had muscles in my arms that were quite well developed because of slinging a hammer all the time.

Today a builder is a manager, and there are about seventy-five different craftsmen who build a home. We just hire a specialist, a sub-contractor to do his specific thing, and then get others to do their specialties. But I don't go to a fitness center to work out. I do not exercise per se. I just stay busy.

I walk around and see a number of properties, in and out of the truck. By moving refrigerators or washers and dryers by myself from one house to another, or rolling the carpeting, hauling off the old carpeting to have the new carpeting put in by the installers, I just stay in shape doing what I do to manage the properties which I own.

I go to an enormous number of Ribbon Cuttings and Ground Breakings each year, both as an ambassador for the Chamber of Commerce and as the Mayor Pro Tem of the City of Springfield. There was a unique opportunity when we went to the Ribbon Cutting to dedicate a portion of the Chesterfield Family Center that had this large climbing rock; we had the opportunity to climb it. I guess it was the Public Information Office that videotaped me going up or down that rock. I hadn't seen the video of my climbing it before the American Red Cross Everyday Heroes Breakfast in March, 2005. I hadn't ever climbed a climbing rock before.

I may walk some with my wife on occasion, particularly on weekends, somewhere pretty: the park near us, Nathaniel Green Park, or around the Greenway Trails that's near here.

My father taught me golf. He was a really good golfer but I had to learn. When I was younger, I could really drive. I could out-drive him, but he could out-score me. My father died at about 80-some years old. I remember that because he could always shoot his age; he'd been a golfer all his life.

I do play golf occasionally. Sometimes it takes about four or five hours to play eighteen holes of golf. And you know, sometimes my work ethic...and I don't really call myself a workaholic...but sometimes I find it a little bit difficult to spend that much time enjoying myself when there's other work I could do that would produce income or give me much more satisfaction than worrying, "Gee, can I get this game over so I can get back to work?" I really have a strong work ethic!

But I do have a nice set of golf clubs and I will play occasionally with my wife and grandsons. They don't play regularly but it's a type of sport that helps them stay in good physical condition. I'm not prejudiced against the game. I can play for nine holes and not have a problem with it, but to go for eighteen holes? There's so much I could be doing! If I could just go buy another piece of property during some of this time, it would make me feel better.

During March Madness, as far as basketball is concerned, I tell this story: my wife is such a basketball fiend that if I were to die during basketball season, she would postpone the funeral until the games were over. That's not true, but we do enjoy basketball.

I was a Drury fan, when I was on the board of trustees there; I'm a Drury alumni! Then when I went to teach at SMS, we went to SMS games. But some of the games were on the same night, conflicting, so I finally just quit Drury's games and went strictly to SMS games. I've been a booster there for over thirty years. We have season tickets for SMS baseball, volleyball, and basketball.

"I love the Missouri State Bears; sometimes the ref's decision stinks!"

We have season tickets for the new Springfield Cardinals baseball team that just started this year, 2005. They even asked me to throw out the starting pitch at one of the games!

Of course we have the grandsons and we go to their games a lot. I like to see people stay in good physical shape so we encourage and help motivate, and we enjoy seeing them develop their skills, too. We go to a lot of baseball and basketball games for the grandchildren.

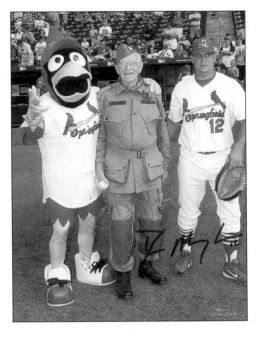

Favorite Food

But as busy as we are, I'd rather have my meals at home. I'm a very common person, a meat-and-potatoes man, along with corn or green beans or breaded tomatoes or macaroni and cheese or pork chops or pot roast. My wife is a good cook, and if I had to pick one favorite, I believe I'd pick pot roast: roast beef with potatoes and carrots, and make sure the gravy that comes from cooking the roast goes on the mashed potatoes. It's just the finest meal I could get anywhere, and I prefer that at home, to the fanciest meals in the finest restaurant in town, with all the fancy sauces and the fancy names.

I also like turkey and dressing. This Stove Top Dressing, to me, is the finest dressing going! I can get dressing at a number of places, whether it's Ziggy's or Perkins or Steak and Ale, but none of it compares with Stove Top Dressing that my wife can make with baked chicken or turkey. I love it!

When we go out to eat, it's not a fancy restaurant. I'm not one for putting on the dog, so to speak. Whether it's a cafeteria where I can pick what I want, or Ziggy's which is a fine little, economical restaurant, it's not the economics that really pleases me, it's the food, the common food, that I enjoy.

I like dessert! I like all types of cakes and pies. I like apple pie better than cherry. I like pecan pie at certain times of the year, particularly the fall. Same way with mince; I love mince pie in the fall of the year. In the spring, I might go for peach or apple. Yes, there is something sweet every night with dinner. Sometimes my wife will make it. For example, these last few days we've had angel food cake and strawberries. And that's fine. Actually, Braum's makes the finest coconut cookies I've ever laid eyes on. When I pass by Braum's and my wife wants ice cream, I nearly always get some of those coconut cookies!

"Jayne and me square dancing in 1951, our second year of marriage."

My wife and I celebrated our 50th wedding anniversary in 2000. We've had a wonderful life together, and our daughters and their families have only made it better.

"Jayne and me in 1985,
in our 35th year of marriage."

"Jayne and me in 1990,
in our 40th year of marriage."

Jayne and me at Hillcrest High School
Jr. ROTC Military Ball March 18, 2005

"Jayne, our daughters, and me, in 2005"

"Jayne and me celebrating our
50th wedding anniversary, in 2000"

Part 6

WWII Reunion Events and Airborne Demonstration Team

It's not that I'm stuck in the past; it's that some of what we read and hear now is opening up the past and providing "the big picture" for those of us who were fighting and weren't able to know at the time.

I try to read everything that I can. Some colleagues have written books about WWII; a number of magazines that I get, like *World War II Magazine*, have stories and information. All that is now being written about the war I find interesting. In addition, some of the movies that have come out provide insights.

I belong to veterans' organizations: the American Legion, Veterans of Foreign Wars, Purple Heart Association. It's good to visit with people who have been in some of the same countries and on the same battlefields, to reminisce and know that they have experienced a similar past. We have a unique bond. At our last Purple Heart meeting, about forty were in attendance. Every month or so another one of our members dies or another needs to go to the Veterans Home in Mount Vernon.

Just last year, 2004, I was asked to go to Lebanon, Missouri, speak at a program, and present a number of men mostly my age with their high school diplomas–sixty years later! I couldn't believe they hadn't received them when they left the school and went to military service. I was so proud to be there!

This May, The Greatest Generations Foundation sent a group of us veterans–all expenses paid–to be part of the 60th Anniversary of Victory in Europe celebration. During nine days we traveled to the WWII Memorial in Washington, D.C., then to Omaha Beach, Utah Beach, and various towns where we'd fought during the Normany battles, with special luncheons and dinners each day, and visits to various cemeteries.

The Greatest Generations Foundation
VETERAN BIOGRAPHY FORM

Please tell us about your service.

Veteran's name: Ralph Kreider Manley

Branch of service: U S Army

Years of military service: 1942-1945

Rank upon discharge: T/5; 6 yrs. later MO Nat'l. Guard
M/Sgt. E8 & Platoon Sgt.

MOS/Specialties: Demolitionist and Radio Operator

Division, Regiment, Company, Platoon, Squad:
101st Airborne Division, 501st Parachute Infantry
Regiment, Demolition Platoon

Foreign countries where you were stationed:
England, France, Holland, Belgium

Medals/honors received:
Bronze Star (2), Purple Heart (5),
CIB. Spearhead (2), Battlestars (4)

Highlights of military service:
Parachuting into France D-Day, 6/6/44;
into Holland 9/17/44;
fighting in Bastogne 12/44-1/45

Please provide brief story of involvement and details significant to your experience while serving in World War II.
After midnight jump on D-Day into enemy stronghold:
House-to-house, street-to-street fighting to take over
towns and areas of the enemy;
Explosives on bridges, locks, railroad, highways to blow if
necessary to keep enemy from going down to reinforce
their troops defending beaches;
Disrupt communications, block and mine all roads going to
beaches, prepare canal locks to blow if necessary, prepare bridges and railroad tracks to blow if necessary,
but save all so we might use them if possible.

One of us veterans died the evening before our return trip home, on The Square in Paris! Nothing worked to revive him. It was probably the best way he could have died, because he was a widower, they'd had no children, and he was with friends. All of us concluded–after he died, of course–what a way to go!

My 501st Airborne Division had a reunion June 2nd through June 4th this year, 2005, in Springfield. My wife, Jayne, and I hosted it. I read a Proclamation in honor of them.

Proclamation

WHEREAS, the 501 Parachute Infantry Regiment (501 PIR) was activated in Toccoa, GA in November 1942; and

WHEREAS, the 501 PIR was a part of World War II's 101st Airborne Division that participated in the invasion of France on June 6, 1944 and the airborne liberation of Holland on September 17, 1944; and

WHEREAS, the 501 PIR made their first jump into Normandy in the early morning hours of D-Day; and

WHEREAS, the 501 PIR was the first regiment into Bastogne, Belgium during the Battle of the Bulge; and

WHEREAS, the 501 PIR bravely parachuted from heights of less than one thousand feet; and

WHEREAS, the 501 PIR received seven awards for distinguished performance on the battlefield; and

WHEREAS, the 501 PIR will be hosting their reunion in Springfield, Missouri, on Saturday, June 4, 2005.

NOW, THEREFORE, I, Ralph K. Manley, Mayor Pro Tempore, of the City of Springfield, Missouri, do hereby recognize the

501 PARACHUTE INFANTRY REGIMENT

for their outstanding service to our Country and encourage all citizens to embrace these soldiers for the dedication they showed in a very difficult time.

IN WITNESS WHEREOF, I have hereunto set my hand and have caused the official seal of the City of Springfield, Missouri, to be affixed this first day of June, in the year of our Lord, two thousand five.

Ralph K. Manley, Mayor Pro Tempore

"I read a Proclamation in honor of them."

Of the veterans themselves, there were no more than seventy. Of those seventy, I will have to admit I'm probably in the best physical shape of anyone. This reunion, if I were guessing, is going to be close to the last. At the banquet Saturday night, June 4, I was given a list to read of those deceased since last year, and there must have been twenty-five. We're going fast!

Infirmities, their age, the crutches, the canes, the wheelchairs. It's sad! I remember these people as young, robust, perfect physical specimens, the best the Army had!

Their spouses, in many cases, are younger. We've had a few that when the soldier died, the spouse remarried, and in several cases she married another former paratrooper, because they had had this friendship from our reunions.

Many of them still smoke, but there was no smoking in the motel and I liked that. They had to go outside. Good! I don't like smoking. But the vast portion of them drink. I do not drink, and never have. I think we spent about seven or eight hundred dollars on liquor, mixers, what have you, for this reunion. My daughter Jennifer and son-in-law Skip helped get the liquor, hauled it in a truck, and set up the bar.

In the hospitality room, where we all gathered, many found it interesting to go over scrapbooks, perhaps a half dozen personal scrapbooks. Some showed a chronology of the veteran: with the uniform on, in between, now. Some had detailed maps of the drop zones or where we landed or where they landed.

It's a lot of work to plan one of these reunions and most of the men are not up to it. There are three of us that probably still are: I'm one, Bill Sefton is another, and then the founder's wife–he died–Glenna Compton Amburgey. The one died who we had scheduled to host for this coming year, 2006. So Glenna Amburgey said, "Well, I'll hold it this next year." Glenna lives in Kentucky. Jayne and I might just as well get ready for another!

The purpose of our reunions is to get together, renew old friendships, and introduce family members. We had a total of 235 people here, which included spouses, children, grandchildren, and about twenty from the WWII Airborne Demonstration Team. We had a first-time event for one of our reunions: a jump by thirteen members of the team which took place at the Springfield Regional Airport.

I'm part of WWII Airborne Demonstration Team, an Oklahoma-based group with members from all over the U.S., who jump in air shows using all World War II-era gear, and still make static line jumps from a vintage C-47 plane.

A parachute with a static line is tied with a string onto the backpack. That's how it opens. We call it a static line jump because that strap gets the jumper clear of the tail of the plane before the chute opens. Typically the plane slows down to a hundred miles an hour, and goes into a slight dive, so that the jumper misses the tail of the plane. When he goes out, he has to go out of the plane a certain way, and keep his feet together, or it may turn the jumper around and it could cause a malfunction in the parachute. The blast from the propellers has a tendency to spin him. All this we were taught with parachute training.

The highlight of this reunion was this plane, seeing the C-47 plane that the veterans could relate to and tell their spouses, children, and grandchildren about. Explain the stripes; explain the colors, perhaps telling that when the war first started, planes were aluminum colored, but later were painted olive-drab; describe incidents.

There are no luxury seats on these planes, but only a bench on either side, with dips in them to seat each person. There are seat belts now, because it can get pretty rough when flying low.

Many of the veterans at our reunion had not seen a jump like this, and most of their spouses and children hadn't either. That's why it was so meaningful to have this done.

The Demonstration Team calls jumps like this a "Hollywood Jump." A Hollywood Jump is one without equipment.

On D-Day, I weighed 180 pounds, but with all my equipment I weighed 417 pounds. For that D-Day jump we were loaded to capacity; they wanted us to take all that was going to be necessary, because, frankly, they weren't even sure that we were going to be able to stay, but they didn't tell us that.

Normally on a training jump, there might be five or as high as ten percent injured with broken legs or sprained ankles or concussions. A daytime jump is much safer because we could see where we were going. For example, the Holland jump–open fields, no flooded areas, no trees, and no enemy.

But on the D-Day jump, just shortly after midnight, all Hell broke loose because we had to go past the coast, with all the guns, before we could get to the area where we were going, seven miles or so behind the lines. And on night jumps, there might be fifteen to twenty percent injured, because of landing in trees, in water, on rooftops, church steeples, with all the heavy equipment.

This reunion jump brought all these stories out for the families, and it was really the highlight of this reunion.

The Springfield Regional Airport shut down for fifteen minutes so that no other planes could land, during the jump. The Airborne Demonstration Team jumped at about a thousand feet and the wind was a little stronger than what we would have liked. When the wind gets above fifteen miles an hour, it's probably safe not to jump because this invites injuries. I think we had gusts up to twenty-two miles an hour, but they wanted to go ahead and jump because of the tremendous effort and expense involved. If we didn't jump then, we would have bused all those people out to the airport just to turn around and go back to the motel. So they said, "It's a little bit risky but we're going to go ahead and jump." The jump turned out fine; we had just one injury and that was a three-point landing: his feet, his ass, and his head!

There could have been some scrapes, because with the wind blowing, it would have a tendency to drag with the chute blowing. So the first thing to do would be to pull on one side of the chute to deflate it, so it can't drag, then turn away from the wind and fold the chute up.

On Hollywood Jumps or training jumps, each one drops with a parachute bag so the jumper can fold his parachute up and put it in the bag. On a wartime jump, we didn't bother: we just left it there.

In combat, our reserve chute on the front was twenty-four feet and white, and our back one was twenty-eight feet and camouflaged. When we jumped so low, as we did, there would be no chance of using our reserve chute but it helped us psychologically.

Originally the chutes were made out of silk, but after we began war with Japan–where the silk came from–there was no more silk and the chutes became nylon. The silk parachute was the easiest one; it had more spring and bounce to it. The nylon chute had more spring than the rayon chute, so the rayon chute was only used for equipment. All the parachutes now are nylon, not silk. The nylon does not rot. The thing that causes nylon to rot is open sunlight; if it's buried in the dirt or soil for years, it doesn't rot.

Even today, when we visit other countries for reunions, we can see what the villagers made when they took the parachutes home: wedding dresses, bedspreads, and draperies made out of the reserve white parachutes.

In the army after they've used one for five years, they sell it as surplus. That's where our Airborne Demonstration Team gets the parachutes we use, from the army as surplus.

The Airborne Demonstration team has riggers who pack the chute for us. They're qualified, and each one has to put his little card or approval sheet in the parachute, so we know who packed it and when. And it needs to be packed within six months of a jump or it has to be packed again.

The C-47 plane is privately owned by a doctor and his wife. We jumpers have to sign a release clause saying we will not hold them liable. Therefore, we did not want to fly the veterans' families, or even the veterans, in that plane.

After World War Two, the American Army sold this plane to England. England used it for years, then sold it to Israel. Israel used it for years, and then this doctor from Oklahoma bought it on EBay. It's been reconditioned, has had all the repairs, all the inspections, and the engine and all have met FAA regulations; both the plane and pilot have to pass all that. It still has its number. That plane was made in Oklahoma City during World War Two. It actually made a D-Day drop, as well as a Holland drop, but then afterwards was sold to England.

When we went to Europe last year, 2004, with the Airborne Demonstration Team, we rented another plane there, another C-47 like this one, also privately owned. There's still a few of them around and they're like a Model-A Ford. There's no luxury on them at all, but they just keep running and running and running. It was cheaper to rent one in Europe than to take this one over, because it would have had to make some fuel stops. Incidentally, the pilot had a charge against him so if he landed in a certain country–in this case France–they might pick him up for the charge he had. So he didn't land there; he just dropped us out and went back to ...wherever! What the charge was, I had no idea.

The jump this year was the first for my family! I was glad for my wife and my children. They had seen the plane in movies but not actually on the ground where they could go in and look around. The airport had a nice moveable stairway that they provided to allow us to get up into it. The typical ladder to get into that plane has only two steps on it, and the first one is about three feet off the ground! Their typical first comment was: "Gosh, this is what you had to fly in?" They weren't made for comfort.

Four movies, *The Longest Day, A Bridge Too Far, Saving Private Ryan,* and *Band of Brothers*–all of those are ones that used C-47s in order to relate what it was like, the best they could. They were about as true as anyone can get.

The movie *Saving Private Ryan* is based on the true story of a man I served with named Frederick Niland–we called him Fritz–who had three or four brothers killed. After Normandy, I was in G Company and he was in H Company, of the 501. One

RESOLUTION

RECOGNIZING MAYOR PRO TEM RALPH K. MANLEY FOR HIS HEROIC
SERVICE TO OUR NATION IN WORLD WAR II AND HIS EXEMPLARY ATTITUDE
AND LEADERSHIP IN OUR COMMUNITY.

WHEREAS, Springfield Zone 3 City Councilman and Mayor Pro Tem Ralph K. Manley
honorably served his nation during World War II as a paratrooper in the 101st Airborne Division of
the U.S. Army; and

WHEREAS, Ralph K. Manley participated in the Allied Forces landing at Normandy,
France, when he jumped from a burning C-47 transport plane at 12:23 a.m. on June 6, 1944; and

WHEREAS,

WHEREAS, Ralph K. Manley will return to the beaches of France for a parachute jump to
re-enact the landing at Normandy for the 60th anniversary of D-Day on June 6, 2004.

NOW, THEREFORE, BE IT RESOLVED BY THE CITY COUNCIL OF THE CITY OF
SPRINGFIELD, MISSOURI, as follows:

That the City Council salutes Mayor Pro Tem Ralph K. Manley for his heroic service to our
nation in World War II and his exemplary attitude and leadership in our community, and wishes him
a safe and fulfilling journey to France.

Passed at meeting: May 24, 2004

Thomas J. Carlson, Mayor

"Springfield Mayor Carlson publicized my return to Normandy for the 60th
anniversary of D-Day on June 6, 2004 at which I was scheduled to jump
with the Airborne Demonstration team."

of the things that I experienced when I've returned to France or Holland, even this year: I remember those buddies that I had–whether killed on D-Day or any other time until the end of the war–as the young men they were at that time. That's how I still relate to them. As I stand in the beautiful cemeteries beside those crosses and see their names, tears come, because they did not get to enjoy this sixty years of freedom that I have had. They did not get a chance to raise a family as I have, to develop a talent or to get an education, as I have. And it makes me very sad. But, on the other hand, I'm so thankful.

Recently I was down at Frederick, Oklahoma, with the Airborne Demonstration Team at a former Army bomber base during World War Two. The runways, two of the buildings, a hangar and another building are still there. The City of Frederick has leased the facilities to the Airborne Demonstration Team for a dollar a year.

"Here's a view of us jumpers inside of the plane, ready to take off."

They have Jump School at least twice a year for which they charge about $750 to a $1000; students pay the fees. They're eager because they want to "serve, honor, and respect the memory of the WWII paratrooper." They really are sincere in their efforts. It's a joy to talk with them; they would listen twenty-four hours a day. They have so many questions.

They use the C-47 plane. The doctor and his wife who own the C-47 live in McAlester, Oklahoma. They are both doctors, anesthesiologists, I believe. It's a tax write-off for them. They gave $100,000 for the plane, bought it from Israel, and then had to get it to the U.S. He flies too, and he went with another pilot who's familiar with flying that plane.

Incidentally, they still use Orange, the color of the Dutch Underground, to this day, for identification purposes. When we visited Holland in September 2004, they gave us orange ribbons to put on. Some of the windmills were still in use when we were there. One of the windmills did not have the blades

"Here's a picture of WWII Airborne Demonstration Team
that went to Normandy."

on it, but the 501st is taking up a collection to restore this windmill, to put the blades back and repair it, and restore it as a monument. There is already a monument, by the way, to the 501st, at Veghel, Holland.

Interestingly enough, as we have toured these same battle areas over the last few years, we met young people who were babies then but of course are older now, maybe in their sixties! The adults we met or saw in WWII–they're gone. But their children remember! They have been told their parents' stories, and they are grateful for their liberation from the Nazi Regime. France and Holland and Belgium all looked forward to liberation. Thank goodness our country didn't have to be liberated but thank goodness for the sacrifices we made. I'm so proud to be an American!

"I'm with the pilot of our plane at the Holland airport, before our jump."

"Tom Hanks, the star of *Saving Private Ryan*, and its director Steven Spielberg joined in the celebration."

"In St. Mere, Eglise, France, in June 2004, at the same old café as on the drop zone in 1944."

"At Drop Zone in St. Mere Eglise, France, swapping flags with a French mother and her two children."

"Me, General Richard Myers, Chairman Joint Chiefs of Staff, Richard 'Harry' Hoots, in France. Harry and I are A.D.T. members."

"People and places from the 2004 visit to Normandy, France, and Holland."

"I made a jump with the team in Oklahoma last year, 2004.
The white stripes were put on the planes after the Sicily 'friendly fire'
incident that killed my brother, Roland."

"This is part of Airborne Demonstration Team. I'm in a WWII jump uniform. Next to me, on my right, is Jake McNease. We're the only two WWII paratroopers in the unit. The rest are re-enactors."

"My family and I went over ten years ago, in 1994, but there was not a drop at that time."

Part 7

RECOGNITIONS & AWARDS, PERSONAL RESUME, & SOME THANK-YOU NOTES

Recognitions and Awards

American Red Cross Greater Ozarks Chapter
Everyday Heroes Award, for Distinguished Service 2005

Boy Scouts of America Ozark Trails Council
Distinguished Citizen Award 2005

City of Springfield
Resolution 5/24/2004 in Recognition of Heroic Service
  during WWII and Exemplary Attitude and
  Leadership in Our Community
Proclamation announcing 9/26/2005 as
  Ralph K. Manley Day

Daughters of the American Revolution
Excellence in Community Award 2004

Drury (College) University
Outstanding Alumni 1967
Distinguished Alumni Service Award 1973
Elected, Board of Trustees

Home Builders Association of Greater Springfield
Award of Special Merit for Service as President 1958
50 Years of Service Award 2004
Hall of Fame Award 2000
Builder Member of the Year 1996

March of Dimes
Lifetime Achievement Award 2000

Military Order of the Purple Heart
Distinguished Service Award 2005

Springfield Apartment and Housing Association
Outstanding Contribution Award for 2000

Springfield Business Journal
Economic Impact Awards 2002:
Lifetime Achievement in Business Award

Springfield, Missouri Convention and Visitors Bureau
Diplomat Award 2005

Springfield Public Schools
Ralph K. Manley All Purpose Room, John McGregor
Elementary School dedicated 1/23/2003

Springfield Savings and Loan League
Certificate of Recognition for Unselfish and Loyal
Service, 1981

Strafford High School
Team Player Award for Career Day
Business Educator 2001

World War II Airborne Demonstration Team
Award for Exemplary and Selfless Service to the Cause
of Freedom 2001

American Red Cross

Together, we can save a life

American Red Cross and KY3 present 5th Annual Everyday Heroes Breakfast

Tuesday, March 15, 2005

"Ralph K. Manley All Purpose Room,
John McGregor Elementary School
dedicated 1/23/2003"

Congratulations on your Diplomat Award. Your effort
to preserve military history and strengthen the Air &
Military Museum has been a tremendous help to the
community. We applaud your efforts, and thank you
once again.

You're also a great councilman!

Tracy

Personal Resumé of Ralph K. Manley

Address: 2335 South Golden,
Springfield, Missouri 65807

Telephone: Home (417) 882-7358
Office (417) 889-5909
Fax   (417) 889-5919

Personal: Born October 15, 1923 in Springfield, Missouri
Married Jayne Atteberry Manley in 1950
3 Adult Daughters, 4 Grandsons
Excellent Health

Education: Master of Business Administration,
Drury College, 1969
Bachelor of Arts, Drury College, 1949

Over 50 years of practical experience as an extremely successful businessman, building contractor, real estate broker, financier, and educator. This includes all aspects of planning, administration, budget control, personnel management, public relations, estimating, bidding, and transactions with governmental agencies, as well as educational experience in teaching, curriculum planning and development, and student and faculty recruitment.

Graduate Courses at Harvard and University of Missouri at Columbia.

As An Educator:

Approved instructor by Missouri Real Estate Commission for Pre-licensing courses at Southwest Missouri State University since 1979 and Continuing Education courses since 1985.

1971-1989   Assistant Professor, Instructor-courses in Real Estate, Introduction to Business, and Finance with Southwest Missouri State University for 17 years full-time, three years part-time. Retiring in 1989 as Professor Emeritus.

1969-1974   Lecturer, courses in Public Relations, Business and Society, and Introduction to Business. Recipient of the 1975 award for outstanding service to the Drury Evening College for "love and concern for students." Awarded Outstanding Alumni of Drury College in 1967.

As An Executive:
Licensed contractor, land developer, licensed Real Estate

1945-2005   Broker, investor, financier, farm owner/manager, and Corporate Executive.

Recognized authority and consultant in residential construction and land development, having built more than 1,500 homes and developed residential subdivisions totaling over 2,000 lots in the Springfield area

Owner and Manager of over 100 real estate properties.

Military Background:
Paratrooper, World War II, 101st Airborne Division, with combat experience in the European Theater of operations. Participated in the D-Day invasion of France, the Battle of Bastogne, Belgium, and saw action in Holland on up to Berlin Germany.
Served in the Missouri National Guard as a Master Sergeant, Instructor, 6 years.
Six times wounded in action and recipient of nineteen decorations-three purple hearts and several medals for gal-

lantry in action and excellence in performance of duty as
a Demolition and Espionage Trooper.
World War II Airborne Demonstration Team

Fraternal Memberships:
United Way Board
Diabetes Association Volunteer
Who's Who in Executives and Professionals
Chamber of Commerce Ambassador
Motivational Speaker for D.A.R.E. Graduations
Life Member of VFW
All Masonic Organizations (32nd Degree Mason)
Abou Ben Adhem Shrine
American Legion 50 Year Member
101st Airborne Division Association Life Member 501st
    Parachute Infantry Association
Home Builders Association of Springfield (50 years)
Springfield Apartment Association
United States Coast Guard Auxiliary (Commander)
Military Order of the Purple Heart Chapter 621,
    Vice Commander of the State Order
Motivational Speaker for over 150 Engagements Yearly

Church:
Member, Elder, Teacher at First and Calvary Presbyterian
    Church since 1966
First & Calvary Foundation Board

City of Springfield & Greene County:
Mayor Pro-Tem of Current 4 year term
Springfield City Councilman Since April, 1999
Vice Chairman Vision 20/20 from beginning to present
Jordan Valley Park Advisory Committee
Metropolitan Planning Organization
Chamber of Commerce Ambassador

Member of Sister Cities
Chairman of Public Involvement Committee
Council Representative on Finance Committee
Member of Planning and Zoning Commission for 5 years
Served on various committees for Building Code updating
Served on Greene County Building Commission for years
Served on Greene County Planning and Zoning
    Commission for its initial adoption
Board Member, Ozark Counseling Center
Board Member, Better Business Bureau

915 East Elm Street, Apt. 301
Springfield, MO 65806

March 14, 2005

Ralph Manley
Ralph K. Manley & Co. Real Estate
1341 West Battlefield
Springfield, MO 65807

Dear Mr. Manley:

I would like to start by thanking you for coming to my Marketing Yourself class on
March 8th, 2005. It showed how dedicated you are to encouraging others and that you
truly enjoy what you do. I must say, I was truly amazed at the energy you possessed and
your incredibly positive attitude that stood out in everything you said.

Not only did you put a smile on my face for the entire hour that you spoke, but you also
gave me confidence to try and be more positive with every obstacle that life may throw
my way. I have never listened to anyone speak with such passion and praise. You gave
me a sense of accomplishment in what I am doing and made me realize that I too can be
successful in all that I do if I work hard and strive to be the best.

You definitely changed my outlook on life in the short time that you were visiting and I
truly thank you for that. Also, thank you so much for the silver dollar that you gave to
me. I will save it and think of your wonderful words of encouragement every time I look
at it.

Sincerely,

Candice L. Radmer

---

821 South Avenue, Apt. B309
Springfield, MO 65806
March 6, 2003

Mr. Ralph Manley
1341 West Battlefield
Springfield, MO 65807

Dear Mr. Manley:

Thank you for speaking at our night class this past Tuesday. Your enthusiasm for life
was invigorating. It made me feel energetic for the rest of the evening.

Specifically, I admire how well you've kept the promise you made during WWII. You've
obviously dedicated your life to helping others in many ways. I find it amazing that
you've built so many homes in Springfield. Moreover, I find it remarkable that you've
volunteered with more than 15 local organizations.

Thank you again for taking time to speak to our class. I only hope my life can provide
me with as much fulfillment.

Sincerely,

Thomas F. Guyer

5705 S. Dayton
Springfield, MO 65810
February 5, 2003

Dear Mr. Ralph Manley:

Thank you so much for taking the time to come to our class on Tuesday night. All I can say is "WOW"! How refreshing you were in this life of turmoil and uncertainty. If only more people, including me, could be half as inspiring and positive as you.

I am currently enrolled in my last semester with SMSU. My major is marketing with an emphasis in sales. I am planning on possibly relocating to Denver. I am very excited about getting out there in the business world. You've inspired me to fight harder for what I want to achieve. You have also made me realize that life could be so much more difficult than I have it.

Again, I appreciate your witty and motivational speech. It has been my pleasure to have the opportunity to meet you. I hope to have the possibility to chat with you again. I wish you the best of luck in all the future challenges you look to conquer.

Respectfully,

Nicole R. Conway

Nicole R. Conway

---

623 W. McGee St.
Springfield, MO 65807
March 15, 2005

Mr. Ralph Manley
Ralph K. Manley & Co. Real Estate
1341 W. Battlefield
Springfield, MO 65807

Dear Mr. Manley:

Thank you for taking time out of your evening to renew my excitement toward my eventual new career (Southwest Missouri State University *Marketing Yourself* class, March 8, 2005).

I've always felt that I display a child-like enthusiasm and animation; I've also worried that, at times, I may be seen as immature instead of passionate! Over the past couple of years, I have let my enthusiasm dim and my confidence dwindle. As I watched and listened to you have such fun, I realized how much I miss my former self and decided it is time for a perpetual encore.

Thanks to you, Mr. Manley, I have put enthusiasm back on high priority and am anticipating an immediate comeback. Never again will I see enthusiastic excitement as immature and, hopefully, I should again be on everyone's give-it-a-rest list . . .

Enthusiastically,

Sheri L. Gibe

Sheri Gibe

P.S. Volunteering is a large part of who I am: "I don't have a life, so I may as well give someone else one." Sheri L. Gibe

5/18/05

Dear Mr. Manley,
You have great stories about the war.
I bet it was scary. My favorite
part of your storie was when you told
us about the flaming plane you had
to jump out of. My other favorite was
when you got a manacure, petecure,
shave, and a hair cut.

sincerly,
Caleb Helgerson

P.S. Good luck on your book.

May, 18, 2005

Dear Mr. Manley,

I really enjoyed your speech yesterday. I thought it was very exciting.
I like the way you chose to be a paratrooper.

Oh! Thanks for the silver dollar. My mom
says you told her you gave away 21,000 of
them. Thats allot of money.

Was it scary being in D-Day? I feel bad
for your twin brother. Was it hard to lose
him?

Well bye.

Sincerely,
Seth Fredrickson

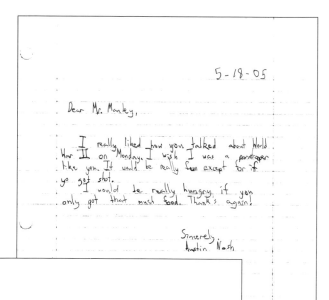

5-18-05

Dear Mr. Manley,

I really liked how you talked about World War II on Monday. I wish I was a paratrooper like you. It would be really fun except for if yo got shot. I would be really hungry if you only got that much food. Thank's again!

Sincerely,
Austin Nash

308 S. Campbell Ave.
Springfield, MO 65806

March 15, 2005

Mr. Ralph Manley
Ralph K. Manley & CO Real Estate
1341 W. Battlefield
Springfield, MO 65807

Dear Mr. Manley:

Thank you very much for coming to Dr. Pettijohn's Marketing Yourself class last Tuesday. I sincerely enjoyed listening to you speak. Your positive outlook on life is inspirational. Your speech lifted my spirits, and most definitely left me with a feeling that I am capable of achieving my highest aspirations.

I personally would like to thank you for my silver dollar. I showed it to all of my roommates when I got home that night. Of course, this was after I told them it was a gift from a World War II Veteran that still jumps out of an airplane once a month! I understand, after talking with you, that you feel this keeps you young. I definitely believe you because you have more zest for life than many kids my age.

In addition to thanking you for my silver dollar, I would like to thank you for being so candid with the details of your life story. After listening to you speak about your experience in World War II and starting your own company, I feel that there is no good reason I can't achieve my goals.

Thank you again for speaking to my Marketing Yourself class. You are a person that has achieved quite a bit in your life, and recognizes the importance of giving back to your community. These qualities make you an excellent role model. I appreciate you taking time out of your schedule to inspire a younger generation!

Sincerely,

Amy O'Neill
Amy O'Neill

Conclusion

Anything is possible in America! Anyone with perseverance can achieve whatever goal he sets his mind to, but he has to have the dream first. And remember: honesty and dreams go together like peaches and cream.

A manager's job is to help other people who also want the chance to grow and achieve, and to persuade them to work when the work needs to be done, how the work needs to be done, for the price the manager wants to pay. Great managers give people jobs, treat them fairly, and give them a chance to share in the wealth because, of course, the manager's primary job is to make a profit. Otherwise, he and his people are out of business. Profit is not a nasty word!

By leveraging my time and my money and by understanding and getting along with other people, I have accomplished great things as a manager and business owner. I have been able to put many people into the building business. I didn't consider them as competition! It was an opportunity for them to grow.

If a person is greedy, perhaps always wanting more than he can afford, how unhappy he is. He gets on the treadmill of debt, is stuck in a job he can't quit because he has to meet those monthly payments, and might work all his life at some job he doesn't enjoy, missing life's pleasures and true contentment.

If he would only save some of whatever he makes, he wouldn't have to go to the credit card! Then he can take advantage of our country's many opportunities.

To see Americans during WWII buckle down and make sacrifices to preserve our freedom was seeing patriotism in its purest form. It was a joy to be a part of this! I don't want another war, but I do want the patriotism and the ability to make sacrifices for a greater good!

The negativity we get in the media is disheartening and almost has a person saying, "Is life worth living? Is America worth living in?" Well, you bet it is! I look for the good things, so that's all I see. That's all I want to see. There's plenty of bad out there; there'll always be! To look for the good things keeps me happy, keeps me optimistic that there is a better way. And, really, a better way is what made America the greatest power on earth.

But to have trust and faith in America, a person needs to have it in himself. Then he can have it in others.

I hope my story shows that, having seen the worst of things and having seen the best of things, I prefer the best of things. I prefer America and those who dream big dreams and search for a better way. And I'm thankful for them all.

RKM

Things to be thankful for...

...the mess after the party, because it means I've been surrounded by *my friends*

...the taxes I pay, because it means that *I am employed*

...the clothes that fit a little too snug, because it means that *I have enough to eat*

...a lawn that needs mowing, windows that need cleaning, and gutters that need fixing, because it means *I have a home*

...the spot I find at the far end of the parking lot, because it means *I am capable of walking*

...all the complaining I hear about our government, because it means *we have freedom of speech*

...the lady behind me in church who sings off key (or the guy at the game who yells too loud), because it means *I can hear*

...my huge heating bill, because it means *I am warm*

...the alarm that goes off in the early morning, because it means *I'm alive*

...the piles of laundry and ironing, because they mean *my loved ones are near by*

...all of the heartaches, stresses, and frustrations my children add to my life, because they mean *I was able to have them and they are alive*

...weariness and aching muscles at the end of the day, because it means *I have been productive.*

(Author unknown)